YOU WANT US TO DO WHAT?

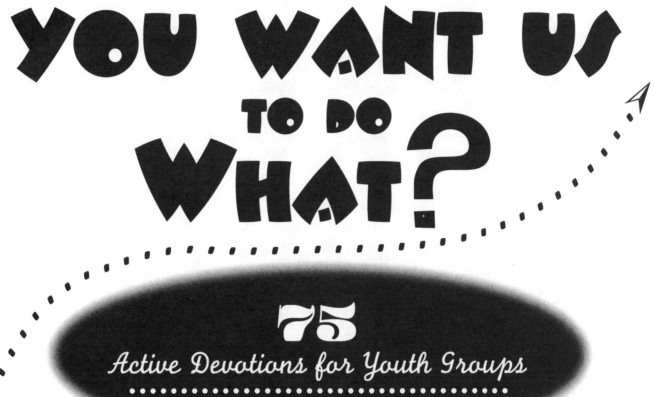

75
Active Devotions for Youth Groups

Mike Gillespie

CPH®
SAINT LOUIS

02 03 04 05 06 07 08 09 10   10 09 08 07 06 05 04 03 02 01

CONTENTS

INTRODUCTION

God's grace speaks powerfully to young people. They hunger for Good News and the power and counsel of God's Holy Spirit. Through youth groups they find a message of hope among friends in faith. When presented with the unashamed claims of the Gospel, teenagers respond with enthusiasm and commitment.

The devotions in this book present the Gospel message in new forms. They invite teens to actively experience the wonderful Good News of Christ. Most of these vignettes need no special materials or preparation. The focus is on the message of Scripture.

Each devotion follows a similar outline. A title, main idea, Scripture reference, and list of materials begins each study. The introduction gets the group involved in the topic. The activity section grabs participants in an active exploration of the theme. The debriefing section shapes the message and helps young people apply Scripture to their lives. Prayer is a most appropriate closure.

Adults or youth can lead these devotions. Directions are clear and precise. Themes are focused around the contemporary issues of teenage life. They maximize discussion and faith exploration.

It is my prayerful hope that these devotions become a window for God's grace for you and the young people you serve. May the uplifting power of the Holy Spirit bless you and your ministry.

Mike Gillespie

YOU WANT US TO DO WHAT?

MAIN IDEA   God, through His Word and Sacraments, strengthens our faith and gives us courage to face difficult situations.

SCRIPTURE   Exodus 14:21–31; 1 Thessalonians 5:9–11

SUPPLIES   Chairs, paper, and pencils.

INTRODUCTION   Have the group pile all the chairs to make a long, tall obstacle in the center of your meeting area. Sit in front of this mountain of chairs.

Tell the story of the Exodus when Moses led the people of Israel out of Egypt, through the desert, to the edge of the Red Sea, where they could go no farther. Pretend the chairs are that sea.

Say: **Suddenly, the people looked around and saw the Egyptian chariots bearing down on them. Surely they would all be killed. There was no place to go for safety. It was an impossible situation.**

ACTIVITY   Appoint someone to be Moses. Ask him to stand before the chairs with raised arms. Read Exodus 14:21–22.

Have the group remove several chairs to make a passage to the other side of the room. When the way is clear, walk everyone through and, like the people of Israel, celebrate.

Divide the group into teams of three or four and give them paper and pencils. Tell them to make up a cheer for Moses. (For example, "Moses, Moses, he's our man. If he can't do it, no one can.") Share the cheers.

DEBRIEFING

- What do you think the Israelites were thinking when they were trapped between the sea and the enemy?

- Who rescued the people—Moses or God? Rewrite your cheers to reflect God's power.

- Describe a recent time when you felt you were facing an impossible situation. What happened?

Sit in a circle and read 1 Thessalonians 5:9–11. Remind everyone that Jesus overcame the great obstacle of our sin, and He continues to use His power in our lives as we face situations impossible to handle on our own.

Say: **We believe with all our heart that God is on our side and can help us get through serious circumstances. God listens to our prayers for faith, courage, and strength. As we study God's Word, the Holy Spirit can lead us to answers and understandings we didn't recognize before. That is God's promise to us.**

Point out that God also wants to work through each participant to bring the hope and encouragement of Christ's power and love to friends facing impossible situations.

PRAYER STARTER   Pray that God will lead you to recognize and be assured of His great power to help.

LOST AND FOUND

MAIN IDEA   No matter how alone or afraid we feel, Jesus is with us and can rescue us.

SCRIPTURE   Luke 15:3–7

SUPPLIES   A long rope and blindfolds.

INTRODUCTION   Ask participants to describe times when they were lost. What happened? How did they feel? Say: **All of us get lost, or feel lost, at times. We take a wrong turn in the car. We feel lost emotionally after someone yells at us or we make a mistake. And we can feel lost spiritually when we don't think God is with us.**

ACTIVITY   Ask participants to put on the blindfolds. Check to make sure no one can see. Line everyone up in a straight line and help them hold onto the rope. Tell everyone that you are going to lead them and get them lost. Lead the group to another room.

DEBRIEFING   Sit in a circle with blindfolds still on. Ask group members where they think they are. Ask them to compare the experience they just had with the feelings they have when they are lost. Read Luke 15:3–7 and discuss:

- Who do you think the shepherd is in this story?

- Whom might the lost sheep represent?

- Describe a time when you felt lost from God.

- Describe a time you felt alone or lost and asked Jesus for help.

- How does God work through you to help minister to lost people?

Ask participants to take off the blindfolds. Sit in a circle, still holding the rope. Talk about the power God's presence has in our lives as He comes to us in His Word and Sacraments. Say: **God's Holy Spirit is our constant companion. Jesus stands ready to rescue us, even when our sin causes us to feel lost and worthless. Through the power of forgiveness Jesus won for us on the cross, nothing can make Him withdraw His shepherding love.**

Use the rope to illustrate the spiritual unity Christians enjoy with Jesus in their midst. Challenge group members to watch for people who seem lost. Christ will work through members to help others who need to hear the Good News of His redeeming work on the cross.

PRAYER STARTER   Thank Jesus for remaining at the center of your youth group and keeping you close to Him.

PUT ON A HAPPY FACE

MAIN IDEA The sadness and grief of sin are replaced by the joy of forgiveness we have through the cross of Christ.

SCRIPTURE 2 Corinthians 5:17, 21

SUPPLIES Two large construction-paper circles for each person, marking pens, tape, and a happy-face sign on a trash can.

INTRODUCTION Hand out paper circles and marking pens to everyone. Ask them to draw a sad face on one side and on the back, write something they did that hurt someone. (For example, someone may have started some gossip about a classmate.) Share comments. Say: **When we sin, we feel separated from God. When we recognize our sin, we feel sad.**

ACTIVITY Hand out the other blank circle. Ask everyone to draw a happy face on one side and on the back, write what Jesus did so that we might have forgiveness.

Read 2 Corinthians 5:17, 21. Ask the group to explain what they think these verses mean. How does God's forgiveness change our sadness to joy? Tell everyone to tear up their sad faces and throw them in the trash can. Each person should read what's on the back of his or her happy face and tape it to the trash can.

DEBRIEFING
- How does it feel to get rid of the sad face caused by sin?

- How can you share your joy?

- If God's love is free and unconditional, why do we ask for His forgiveness for our sins?

Remind the group that Jesus came to be the complete sacrifice for our sins. What He did on the cross was done for each of us. His love is so great He was willing to save us with His very own life. The sadness of the crucifixion is replaced by the happiness of Easter. Jesus calls us to repentance and faith—He leads us to turn from our old sinful ways and enables us to live as God's people.

Challenge the group to memorize the Bible verses, remembering that Christ has the power to turn the sad face of sin to the happy face of God's forgiveness.

PRAYER STARTER Confess your continuing need for forgiveness. Thank God that you have this forgiveness through the cross of Christ.

SOUR DEALS

MAIN IDEA   When we have a bad experience that leaves us feeling rotten inside, Jesus' love and power can bring about change.

SCRIPTURE   Matthew 26:69–75; John 21:15–19

SUPPLIES   A lemon wedge and a cookie for each person.

INTRODUCTION   Sit in a circle and ask group members to describe something that happened in the past week that they would describe as a "sour deal." For example, they were grounded or a parent went back on a promise to let them do something. Share responses.

Say: **Life is full of sour deals—those experiences that make us feel rotten inside. We walk away knowing things just aren't right.**

ACTIVITY   Give each person a fresh lemon wedge to eat. Say: **While you're sucking on this sour lemon wedge, I'm going to read an experience from Peter's life that was a very sour deal.** Read Matthew 26:69–75. Discuss:

● Why do you think Peter did what he did?

● How was Peter's experience like eating a lemon?

● How do you think you would have felt if you had been Peter?

Say: **This would have been one sour deal for Peter if Jesus had left him there. But He didn't. Jesus went directly to Peter. Jesus also comes to you when you need to recover from a sour deal. Through the power of the Holy Spirit working through His Word and Sacraments, Jesus calls you to repentance, to faith, and to live as His child.**

DEBRIEFING   Gather in a circle and have someone read John 21:15–19. Give each person a cookie to eat. Talk about how amazed Peter must have been to find out that Jesus still loved him. Jesus turned Peter's bad experience into an opportunity to minister to him. Jesus had work for Peter to do, so He forgave him, empowered him, and enabled him to do that work.

Tell the group that Jesus will never stop loving them either. Like Peter, they become the hands, feet, heart, and voice that shares God's love and tells others of His salvation. Discuss ways Jesus can help them in their daily lives, turning their sour deals into something sweet (like that cookie!).

PRAYER STARTER   Praise God that He can bring something good out of sour situations.

STRETCHER BEARERS

MAIN IDEA The loving friendship of Jesus leads us to work together as friends in Christ.

SCRIPTURE Mark 2:1–12

SUPPLIES A heavy blanket or a canvas stretcher.

INTRODUCTION Ask each person to think about his or her three best friends. Discuss times when friends have helped group members out of tough situations. Say: **When we need help, we often go to our best friends. We know we can count on them to help us out. Jesus met some people one day who wanted to help their friend. It was quite an experience.**

ACTIVITY Put the blanket (or stretcher) in the center of the group. Have a volunteer lie down on it. Ask one group member to grab one corner and try to pick the person up. (He or she won't be able to.) Add another person (on a different corner). See if they can lift, not drag, the person safely. Add a third person and then a fourth. Ask the group of four to gently carry the person around your meeting area. Discuss what this suggests about teamwork.

DEBRIEFING Read Mark 2:1–5. Discuss:

- Jesus recognized the faith of the friends. In your own words, tell what they must have believed.

- What was the paralyzed man's first and greatest need? What is yours?

- Describe a time you and other friends worked together to help someone.

Say: **Friendships are important to all of us. Sometimes we need our friends to help us; we shouldn't be afraid to ask for that help. Working together, friends can sometimes do a lot more than if each one goes it alone.**

Jesus noticed something important when that man was lowered before Him. His care and that of the friends extended beyond the man's physical needs. Jesus first spoke of the faith of the man's friends and then healed the man's sinful condition with forgiveness.

Consider what that means. God can work through you and your believing friends to lead someone to the blessings of His Word of salvation. Who do you know right now that needs that kind of help? Trust Christ to show you and your friends where to minister.

PRAYER STARTER Bring the needs of a friend to Jesus in prayer.

MAIN IDEA   We praise the name of Jesus who is Lord and Savior.

SCRIPTURE   Philippians 2:9–11; Acts 4:12

SUPPLIES   18" lengths of yarn, marking pens, and poster board cut into 8½" × 5½" name cards for each person. Punch holes in the top corners of the name cards.

INTRODUCTION   Say: **All of us have a name that's going to be with us for the rest of our lives. I'd like each of you to make one statement about your name. You can say anything you'd like.** Share responses.

ACTIVITY   Pass out yarn, marking pens, and name cards. Ask each person to write his or her first name down the left side of the card. After each letter, ask them to write a word or phrase that describes them and starts with that letter.

On the other side of the card, have them write the name *Jesus* down the left side. After each letter, ask them to write words or phrases that describe Jesus and start with that letter.

String the yarn through the holes in the poster board and wear the name cards. Share the responses.

DEBRIEFING

- What made it difficult to find words to describe yourself?

- What was different when you thought about Jesus' name?

- Why is Jesus' name so powerful? (Read Acts 4:12.) What are we saved from? What are we saved for?

- Why is it significant that we pray in Jesus' name rather than our own name?

Ask someone to read Philippians 2:9–11. Say: **We remember that Jesus' name is above every name. We remember that His name is always more important than our name. We remember to honor that name.**

Ask everyone to kneel. Read the Bible passage again three or four words at a time and ask the group to repeat the phrase.

Say: **As believers, we recognize Jesus Christ is Lord over us. He's Lord of our thoughts and our actions. When we live with Christ as our Lord, we live and act to the glory of God. That's what matters.**

PRAYER STARTER   Ask Jesus to make His name and will known to you and the members of the group.

WEEDS, ROCKS, & GOOD SOIL

MAIN IDEA   Jesus desires that His Word will grow and increase in our lives.

SCRIPTURE   Matthew 13:1–9; 1 Thessalonians 2:13; 2 Timothy 3:14

SUPPLIES   Small rocks, potting soil, and a box of straws.

INTRODUCTION   Ask the group to suggest several things a plant must have to be strong and healthy.

Say: **These are basic things a plant needs to grow strong and healthy. Let's consider what you need to grow strong and healthy spiritually. Let's look at a parable Jesus told.**

ACTIVITY   Give each person a straw and divide the group into three circles. In the center of the first circle is just the hard floor. In the center of the second circle place a layer of rocks. In the center of the third circle place a thick layer of good soil. Tell the group that the straws represent plants, which represent people.

Read Matthew 13:1–9. At the end of each section, tell the group representing that type of soil to plant their straws. (For example, after talking about the seed that fell on the path, the first group would try to get their straws to stand up on the hard floor.) Continue until all three groups have tried to plant their straws.

DEBRIEFING
- How well will the plants grow on the hard path?
- How well will the plants grow in the rocky soil?
- How well will the plants grow in the good soil?
- In what ways do these soil types describe Christians today?
- To think about: Where are you in this picture?

Say: **Picture yourself as a person with rocky or weedy soil. Sins are taking over your life. It's likely that peer pressure and popular opinion would decide your actions. Instead of living to please God, you would live to please others and yourself. You would have no use for Christ and the power He can bring you.**

Who can change this picture? Only Jesus—He died to forgive our sins. He makes us good-soil people that not only hear but also believe, understand, and live His Word. We can do this through the blessing and power of the Holy Spirit as He works in and through the Word of God. That's why it's so important to continue to hear His Word. Read 2 Timothy 3:14 and 1 Thessalonians 2:13 and praise God!

PRAYER STARTER   Pray that God will bless everyone in the group so that all may grow in His Word and increase in faith.

WINNERS

MAIN IDEA   Because of the cross of Christ, we sinners are now winners.

SCRIPTURE   1 Corinthians 15:56–57; Philippians 3:12–14; 4:4–8

SUPPLIES   A whistle and a trophy.

INTRODUCTION   Line everyone up along a starting line in your meeting area. Designate another point as the finish line. When you blow the whistle, participants race each other by walking heal to toe as fast as they can. (If you have a large group, run smaller races or heats. Winners in the heats compete in the final.)

Gather together and cheer the winner. Say: **Wow, it's great to be a winner. That's something all of us want to be. The apostle Paul talked about this in the letter he wrote to the church at Philippi.**

ACTIVITY   Sit in a circle. Pass the trophy around the group. As each person receives the trophy, he or she should tell the group one thing for which he or she would like to receive a trophy. Read Philippians 3:12–14.

DEBRIEFING   ● Why do people like to be winners or do something special to get a trophy?

● How do you feel about people who win all the time and never seem to come in second?

● What goal do you think Paul wants to reach?

● How do you become a winner in God's eyes?

Say: **Life as a Christian! Some people aren't even in the race. Some quit and walk away. We all fall flat on our face—and we do it often. Though some people fall and stay down, we can be sure that Jesus is right there, eager to lift us up with His forgiveness. The Holy Spirit empowers us to continue on, encouraging us through the Word.** Read Philippians 4:4–8.

And one thing we can be certain of—the victory is ours! Read 1 Corinthians 15:56–57. **We don't have to be the fastest, the richest, the smartest, or the toughest. Jesus gives us the final victory, which He won on the cross. Keep your eyes on the prize.**

PRAYER STARTER   Pray that God will keep each of you faithful, in the powerful name of Jesus.

PUBLIC DISPLAYS OF LOVE

MAIN IDEA   It's a fact that God's awesome love for each of us is a free gift of grace.

SCRIPTURE   John 3:16; Romans 5:6–8

SUPPLIES   A large gingerbread cookie with a big heart drawn on it. Make a set of index cards with one word from John 3:16 on each card.

INTRODUCTION   Ask everyone to tell you one thing that a parent did in the past week to display love.

Give each participant one or more of the index cards. Ask the group to reassemble the words of the Bible verse. Do not give any hints.

Once the cards are in order, read the verse. Ask the group what the verse tells about God's love.

ACTIVITY   Sit together in a circle. Pass the gingerbread cookie around the group. Tell each person to break off a piece and then tell one thing he or she did recently to share God's love with someone. (Remind the group that everyone should get a piece of the cookie.)

DEBRIEFING

- Why do you think it's sometimes hard to share love with others?

- What was the greatest act of love someone ever shared with you?

- What's the difference between God's love and human love?

- Why was Jesus the greatest expression of God's love for us? (Read Romans 5:6–8.)

- What did God want us to understand through Jesus about how much we are loved?

Say: **God's love is difficult to understand. The Bible tells us that God loved us so much He sent Jesus to rescue us. God didn't want anything to keep us from knowing Him. He sent Jesus to become one of us. He became sin for us. He was punished for us.**

To know Jesus Christ as our Lord and Savior is to know God's love. It's through Jesus that God's special love can be shared with others.

PRAYER STARTER   Pray that God's love will be made clear to everyone in the group. And pray that more people will hear the Good News of God's love.

THE LADDER TO HEAVEN

MAIN IDEA   Heaven is the final destination for all believers in Christ.

SCRIPTURE   Genesis 28:10–15

SUPPLIES   A stepladder, tape, marking pens, paper.

INTRODUCTION   Sit together in a circle. Ask:

- How many of you would like to go to heaven?

- What's the alternative?

- Where is heaven anyway?

Say: **We all have different ideas of what heaven will be like. Once Jacob had a dream about a stairway that reached to heaven. What does heaven look like in your dreams?**

ACTIVITY   Read Genesis 28:10–15. Give everyone paper and marking pens. Ask them to draw a picture of what they think heaven will look like.

Set up the stepladder in the center of the group. Have everyone climb as high up the ladder as they feel safe and then describe what they have drawn. Then hang their drawings on the sides of the ladder.

DEBRIEFING

- Why do you think heaven is so important to us?

- How do you get to heaven? (See Acts 16:31.)

- Can you be sure you'll get there? (See Ephesians 2:8–9.)

Say: **I asked you to climb *up* the ladder to tell about heaven. Jesus came *down* to earth so that we can go to heaven. It's God's action—in Christ—that obtains heaven for us. What a relief! We can be sure, as believers in His death and resurrection, that heaven is ours. It's a gift from God.**

Remember the stairway in Jacob's dream? God didn't say, "Get busy, Jacob, and start climbing." Reread Genesis 28:15 and identify God's "I" statements. Praise God that He comes to us with His power and blessing.

PRAYER STARTER Pray that God will lead us to live as His people now and in eternity.

FRIENDSHIP IS ...

MAIN IDEA   Jesus is our best friend and our example in building friendships.

SCRIPTURE   John 15:12–14

SUPPLIES   Newsprint and marking pens.

INTRODUCTION Ask everyone to pretend that they have just been nominated for the "Best Friend of the Week" award. Share reasons why they would deserve that nomination.

Say: **Good friendships take a lot of work. There are things we must be willing to do to make our friendships strong. Usually, most of us will have only one or two best friends from among the bunch.**

ACTIVITY   Divide into twos and give each pair a sheet of newsprint and a marking pen. Have one person lie down on the newsprint while the other traces around his or her body. Draw a line down the middle of the outline and label the halves A and B.

Ask each partner to draw five symbols inside half of the body outline that represent qualities that make his or her partner a great friend. They cannot use words.

Share the results. Discuss:

- What do you think is your partner's best quality as a great friend?

- What do you think is your best quality as a good friend?

- What qualities do you think Jesus has that make Him a good friend to us?

DEBRIEFING   Read John 15:12–14. Discuss:

- What's Jesus telling us in the Bible passage?

- Why is it really hard to do what Jesus wants?

Jesus says that the greatest love someone can show is to give his or her life for a friend. That's the love that Jesus—as our greatest Friend and Savior—shows us.

Say: **Friendships are a gift from God. Close friends encourage us and help us keep going. Jesus is like that. He will never give up on us. He gave His life for us so He could call us friend. Let His love guide you in your friendships.**

PRAYER STARTER Pray that Jesus will help the group remember Him as the source of true friendship.

BLESSED ARE THE PEACEMAKERS

MAIN IDEA   Jesus made peace between us and God. His example helps us be peacemakers.

SCRIPTURE   Matthew 5:9

SUPPLIES   Poster board, scissors, marking pens, and yarn for each person; newspapers; and a hole punch.

INTRODUCTION   Sit in a circle and scan your local newspaper together. Ask the group to find headlines and articles that describe people and groups who aren't at peace with one another.

Say: **Fighting and disagreements fill the world. Do you think it's possible to be at peace with one another? What does it mean for you to be at peace with yourself or others? What are some reasons for all the conflict?**

ACTIVITY   Hand out poster board, scissors, marking pens, and yarn. Ask everyone to cut the poster board in half. Punch holes in the top corners of both pieces and attach yarn so it can hang over the shoulders like a sandwich board. Ask everyone to write specific examples of peacemaking on his or her sign beginning with the phrase, "I was a peacemaker when I …" Wear the signs and walk around the room, reading each other's signs.

DEBRIEFING   Sit in a circle and read Matthew 5:9. Discuss:

◑   Why do you think Jesus said peacemakers would be called "sons of God"?

Say, **Sin put us at war with God. Jesus made our peace with God by giving His own life as a sacrifice for our sin. Now, rather than being enemies with God, we are His sons and daughters.**

PRAYER STARTER   Pray that Jesus will help each member of the group be a peacemaker and share the peace that only He can give.

LIVING AS SHEEP

MAIN IDEA	God always takes care of us like a shepherd cares for his sheep.
SCRIPTURE	Psalm 23
SUPPLIES	A long rope. Label six rooms or sections of your meeting area with the signs: **Green Pastures; Quiet Waters; Paths of Righteousness; Valley of Death; Banquet Table; House of the Lord.**
INTRODUCTION	Set up a circle of chairs and put a sign on the outside that says *Sheep Pen.* Gather the group inside and sit down. Say: **For a few minutes you're all going to become sheep. I'm going to ask you some questions. Answer each one by saying "baaaaa" like sheep.**

- Do you ever really, really need something?
- Do you ever feel lonely or afraid?
- Do you sometimes want peace and quiet?

ACTIVITY Ask everyone to stand in a circle. Join everyone together in a line with the rope. Say: **You know, you sheep are very interesting critters. You quietly meander around looking for something to eat, not paying much attention to what's going on. Without a shepherd around, you'd get into lots of trouble. I'm going to be your shepherd and lead you on a journey. Follow me.**

Lead the sheep (joined together by the rope) to each room or area where the six signs are posted. Stop at each one and use these questions or directions.

Green Pastures: Tell everyone to sit down and think about a time when he or she felt very safe. Share responses.

Quiet Waters: What's the difference between the "quiet waters" of life and those times of "raging rapids"?

Paths of Righteousness: How can you tell which is the right path and which is the wrong one?

Valley of Death: What kind of evil might people fear?
What can comfort us?

Banquet Table: If God prepared a banquet table for you, what do you think would be served?

House of the Lord: Where is the house of the Lord?
Who is invited there?

DEBRIEFING Return the group to the *Sheep Pen.* Untie the rope. Read Psalm 23.

Say: **It's an incredible thing to know God as our shepherd. God protects us and loves us and takes care of us. Just like a shepherd takes care of his sheep, our Good Shepherd protects us from the greatest of evils—sin, death, and the devil. He comforts us with the promise of forgiveness, life, and salvation. This is an everlasting promise, sealed when Jesus our Savior died on the cross and arose on Easter!**

PRAYER STARTER Pray that each of you will know God's shepherding love.

PEOPLE FISHING

MAIN IDEA   Jesus asks us to tell others about Him so they also can become His disciples.

SCRIPTURE   Mark 1:16–17

SUPPLIES   A fishing pole with an artificial worm (or a gummy worm) tied to the end, newsprint, and marking pens.

INTRODUCTION   Sit in a circle. Pass the fishing pole around. Ask everyone to share what they think the best way to catch a fish might be.

Say: **People who like to fish try out different kinds of bait and lures to see what will attract different kinds of fish.** Discuss:

- ☻ How do you think fish tell the difference between live bait and artificial lures?
- ☻ Which kind do you think is more effective? Why?

ACTIVITY   Say: **Sometimes people try to "catch" us or convince us to work for their cause, or follow their example, or go along with something they want to do.**

Place newsprint and marking pens in the center of the group. Say: **Be a human fish. On a sheet of newsprint, write down a persuasive phrase or sentence that a friend might say to hook you into doing something.** Discuss with the group:

- ☻ Which approaches are the most effective in getting you to follow a leader, whether to do something right or wrong. Why?
- ☻ What factors do you think about before deciding to go along with a leader?
- ☻ What persuasive approaches are you good at using?

DEBRIEFING   Read Mark 1:16–17. Say: **Jesus called Simon and Andrew to leave their fishing nets and follow Him. He made only one persuasive statement, "Follow Me, and I will make you fishers of men." They immediately left their fishing boats and followed Jesus.**

Jesus calls us, through our Baptism and God's Word, to follow Him and tell others about Him so that they too can be His disciples. God's Holy Spirit promises to give us the courage and the words we need to share His love. Discuss with the group:

- ☻ What would happen if you talked to a friend at school about Jesus?
- ☻ What are some natural and winning ways to witness your faith to friends?
- ☻ Can people see "little Christs" when they look at your actions or listen to your words?

PRAYER STARTER   Ask that each group member be blessed with the ability to share the Good News of salvation in Jesus with others.

HAS IT QUIT STORMING?

MAIN IDEA   Jesus promises to help us get through the emotional storms of life that scare us.

SCRIPTURE   Matthew 8:23–27

SUPPLIES   Candle and matches (or a flashlight), and a teddy bear or some other stuffed animal.

INTRODUCTION Sit in a circle. Pass the teddy bear around the group. As each person receives it, he or she should tell the group the worst storm they remember as a child. What was scary about it? Ask: **What kinds of storms are there other than those in nature?**

ACTIVITY   Go to a room in your church that can be totally darkened. Sit in a circle. Turn out the lights. Tell the group to imagine there's a storm raging outside and the power is out. They are stuck in the darkness. Memorize these questions to ask:

● What kind of "emotional storms" do people sometimes face?

● When we have emotional storms, why might we feel that we're without power?

● When we have emotional storms, why does everything seem dark around us?

● Whom do you want with you when you get stuck in a stormy situation?

DEBRIEFING   Light the candle. Read Matthew 8:23–27. Say: **The disciples thought they were going to die in that sudden storm. They went to Jesus in a panic. With His power He brought immediate calm to the seas. That same calming power is available in your life.**

Jesus is always there to calm those huge, horrible, emotional storms, even when you feel like giving up. Just turn it over to Him. Let Jesus bring calm. He will, you know. Just like that day on the Sea of Galilee, Jesus has power over wind and waves. Just like that day on the cross on Calvary, Jesus has power over sin. Just like that early Easter morning, Jesus has power over death. Just like every day of your life, Jesus has power to calm your anxieties and give you peace.

PRAYER STARTER Pray that God's Holy Spirit will bring calm to those who are facing storms in their lives.

WATCH WHERE YOU BUILD!

MAIN IDEA   When our lives are built on Jesus, we have a sure foundation.

SCRIPTURE   Luke 6:46–49

SUPPLIES   Two sets of building blocks, one regular house brick, and several sheets of paper.

INTRODUCTION   Sit in a circle. Pass around the brick and a wad of paper. Ask each person which one would make the better material for a good, strong foundation. Ask:

- Why would a house or building need a good foundation?

- What might happen if a builder didn't use a good foundation?

ACTIVITY   Divide into two groups. Give each group a set of building blocks. Give one group the paper.

Say: **I want you to build the tallest and strongest structure that you can, using the materials you've been given. Group A will build their structure on the floor. Group B must crumple the paper and use those paper wads as their structure's foundation.** Compare results and talk about the experience. Ask:

- Which of these structures do you think is the strongest right now?

- What's the problem with the one that has a paper foundation?

DEBRIEFING   Read Luke 6:46–49. Say: **A foundation is basic. It holds things together. What is basic in your life? What holds things together? If you are building your life on a weak and shaky foundation of bad values and immoral behavior, then you will probably have lots of problems.**

If your life is built on the foundation of Christ, you are on solid ground. When the times get tough, Jesus will be there to get you through. Without Him, life can crumble to pieces with nothing firm to grab hold of. With Christ, you rest on the firm promises of His forgiveness, love, care, guidance, protection, life, and salvation.

PRAYER STARTER   Pray that God's Holy Spirit will help each of you to build on the solid foundation of Jesus Christ, our Savior.

PACKING UP

MAIN IDEA   In life, we probably will do difficult things, such as leaving our friends and moving to another place. In life we certainly can trust that God will be with us.

SCRIPTURE   Genesis 12:1–4

SUPPLIES   A Bible, a suitcase, paper, and marking pens.

INTRODUCTION   Hand out paper and marking pens. Tell group members to draw or list objects they would take with them if they were going on a long vacation. As they share their ideas, have them put their papers in the suitcase. Place a Bible in the suitcase.

ACTIVITY   Tell the group to pretend they are going on a trip with you. Take the suitcase and walk around your facility. Stop in another room far from your meeting area. Unpack the suitcase. Ask:

- What if I said you could never go back home. How would you feel?

- How long do you think this stuff in the suitcase would help?

- Whom would you miss most? Why?

- Why is it hard when people move?

DEBRIEFING   Read Genesis 12:1–4. Say: **Imagine what packing up and leaving like that must have been like for Abram. God spoke and Abram responded.**

Sometimes we face tough situations such as moving away from our friends. We may feel unsure and uneasy and even unwilling. Abram trusted God in such a situation and God blessed him and his family. Jesus said He would always be with us no matter what was happening. His love for us is so great, He willingly died on the cross for us. Trust Jesus to help you through those tough times. Jesus is near and will bless you.

PRAYER STARTER   Pray that God will always be with you, blessing you, even as you face tough times.

THE SECRET OF CONTENTMENT

MAIN IDEA   Paul says Jesus can help us be content in the circumstances we have to face in life.

SCRIPTURE   Philippians 4:11, 13; 2 Corinthians 11:24–27

SUPPLIES   A long sheet of newsprint, tape, and marking pens.

INTRODUCTION   Ask the group to complete this sentence: "For me, being satisfied, being content, means … " Share responses. Ask:

- When was the last time you remember feeling really content?

- On a scale of one to five, with five the highest, how would you rate your contentment? Explain your rating.

ACTIVITY   Stretch out the long sheet of newsprint on the floor. Place marking pens along the sheet. Ask the group to spread out around the paper and write down as many responses as they can to the phrase: "I'm content when I … "

Hang up the sheet and share responses. Ask what the group thinks can bring a person real contentment.

Read 2 Corinthians 11:24–27. Tell the group the apostle Paul faced all those setbacks. Ask them what they think his contentment rating might have been.

Then read Philippians 4:11, 13. Point out that the same man who was treated so harshly also wrote these words of contentment. Ask them why they think he was content despite unhappy circumstances.

DEBRIEFING   Say: **It's really hard to be content. Discontent is easy. We always seem to want something different from what we have. No matter how tough the circumstances, Paul knew he could lean on Christ to get him through. It was Christ's certainty, not Paul's ability, that led Paul to contentment.**

Ask group members to share one area of their life where they feel the greatest discontent. Ask in what ways the Holy Spirit might help make them more content.

Say: **As long as we are sinners in a sinful world, we'll have problems. Even in difficult circumstances, God can help you change the way you deal with your problems. Paul didn't stop people from being cruel to him. But the way he reacted to the abuse was affected by the power of God working in his life. Through Jesus he had a power that some people didn't understand. Paul could forgive because he was already forgiven. He could see beyond the pain to the blessings God promised. The power of God's love, care, and grace colored his every circumstance. That power is available to each of you.**

PRAYER STARTER   Pray that God's Holy Spirit will work in your lives, especially where there is great discontent. Pray for peace, joy, and contentment.

GIFTS

MAIN IDEA God showed His love by giving us the perfect gift—Jesus, His Son, our Savior.

SCRIPTURE James 1:17; 1 John 4:9–11

SUPPLIES A shoe box, wrapping paper, tape, marking pens, and three sheets of paper for each threesome. On a large banner, write *God Loves You.* Place the banner inside a large box and wrap it.

INTRODUCTION Sit in a circle. Ask group members to pretend that they have just been invited to a friend's birthday party. What gift would they give to make that person very happy? Share responses.

ACTIVITY Divide into groups of three. Give each group a shoe box, wrapping paper, tape, marking pens, and paper. (All groups should have identical wrapping paper.)

Say: **Giving and receiving gifts is an important part of life. I want each of you to think of one gift you would most like to receive at this moment. Draw it on a piece of paper. No words or names. Put your picture in your group's shoe box. Wrap the box as a gift.**

When the small groups finish, mix up the boxes and set them in front of everyone. Ask for a volunteer to unwrap one of the boxes. Tell everyone to keep silent. Display the three pictures and ask people to guess who drew them. Follow this procedure with the other boxes.

DEBRIEFING Read James 1:17. List some of the good gifts from God. Ask the group to guess what's in the big box you have wrapped. Tell them it's the most perfect gift from above.

Let the group open the box. Unfold the banner and hang it up. Say: **Knowing that God loves you with a love so big that nothing can take it away is the best gift you'll ever receive.**

Read 1 John 4:9–11. Say: **God gave us the perfect gift to demonstrate His love. That was the gift of our Lord and Savior, Jesus Christ. Let's never stop thanking God for His love in Jesus.** Ask:

- What makes Jesus the best and most perfect gift?

- How can we share the gift of God's love with others?

PRAYER STARTER Pray that group members will share God's love with others during the week.

YOU DESERVE AN AWARD

MAIN IDEA We are God's redeemed, loved, and blessed people who are individually unique and special.

SCRIPTURE Psalm 8; Romans 8:38–39

SUPPLIES Draw a trophy design and photocopy it on heavy paper for each person. Crayons and masking tape.

INTRODUCTION Ask group members to describe one thing that is special about their families or an individual family member. Ask:

- What makes someone special?

- How do you get to be special?

ACTIVITY Give each person a trophy picture, crayon, and a piece of masking tape. Tell them to tape the picture to their back. Ask everyone to move around the room and write something special about each person on the trophy hanging on their back.

Gather together and have people read some of the comments written about them. Ask:

- Which comments surprise you?

- Why is it sometimes hard to think of yourself as special in those ways?

DEBRIEFING Say: **Sometimes we doubt that we're any good. We see the wrong things we do, the mistakes we make, our sinful attitudes. Sometimes we think others have been given all the talent, all the good looks, all the best parents, and on and on. We forget that God has done mighty things for us and in us. You see, through the saving power of Jesus and the renewing power of the Holy Spirit, He has made us His own people.**

Read Psalm 8. Say: **Psalm 8 says that God has crowned each one of us with glory and honor. He restored us through Christ. There is nothing more special than that.**

Ask the group how they think God feels when one of them thinks or feels he or she isn't special.

Read Romans 8:38–39. Say: **You are special. Each one of you is a child of God and no one can ever take that from you. No circumstance or situation can separate you from God's love. God made you His child—you are special indeed.**

PRAYER STARTER Thank God for the uniqueness of each person in the group and for the special love He gives to His special people.

SURPRISE!

MAIN IDEA   One of the great surprises in this world is God's continuing love—share the news and the love with others.

SCRIPTURE   Romans 5:7–8; 1 Corinthians 10:31

SUPPLIES   A dollar bill for each person, an inflated balloon, and a pin.

INTRODUCTION   To get everyone's attention, pop the balloon. Say: **Most of you really jumped. You were surprised. Surprises in life are important. They keep things interesting.**

ACTIVITY   Say: **I'm going to do something else that's going to surprise all of you.** Give everyone a dollar bill. Ask for any reactions. Discuss:

- Why do we need surprises in our lives?

- How do you usually respond when a surprise comes your way?

- What surprising things have happened to you lately?

DEBRIEFING   Say: **Jesus was a big surprise to many people. No one was expecting the promised Messiah to die on a cross. But His love is so surprisingly great that He willingly was punished for us sinners.** Read Romans 5:7–8. **And surprise of surprises, we can live for Him and share His love, as the power of the Holy Spirit works in us.**

Read 1 Corinthians 10:31. Say: **The Bible verse says to do everything to the glory of God. Even surprises can be to the glory of God. I'd like you to use your dollar bill to surprise someone with kindness. This is a chance to do something creative that shows kindness to another person. Even a single dollar bill can bring surprising joy. You decide how to do that. And then give God the glory.**

PRAYER STARTER   Pray that God will encourage each group member to show a special surprise of kindness to someone.

R-E-S-P-E-C-T—YOUR PARENTS

MAIN IDEA   God wants us to respect our parents. We need God's forgiveness for our past disrespect and His power for our present and future actions.

SCRIPTURE   Ephesians 6:1–3; Ephesians 4:32

SUPPLIES   Paper, pens, envelopes, and stamps.

INTRODUCTION   Give each person several sheets of paper and a pen. Ask everyone to complete this statement as many times as they can think of an answer (one answer per sheet of paper): "I show disrespect when I …"

Gather in a tight circle. Tell the group to wad up their sheets of paper. Tell them to throw the paper wads at other people in the circle at the appointed signal. Everyone should stop when you signal again. Discuss:

- What happened during that experience?
- What were you throwing?

Ask volunteers to unwad some of the sheets of paper and read the answers to the group.

Say: **Disrespect seems to be the "in" thing these days. We get it thrown at us, so we want to give it back. People don't seem to have much respect for themselves, for their teachers, for their parents, or for others. What's happening? What's going on?**

ACTIVITY   Read Ephesians 6:1–3. Ask each person to think of his or her parents as just regular people who make mistakes, who have wants and needs, including the need for forgiveness. Ask: **How can you be kind and understanding and forgiving to your parents even when they don't seem kind and understanding and forgiving to you?**

Discuss and then read Ephesians 4:32. Say: **We can be kind and understanding and forgiving because Christ has already done this for us and helps us to do this for others.**

Give each person a blank sheet of paper. Ask everyone to write a letter to one or both of their parents. Ask them to write in a respectful way that would really help build that parent up. Suggest that they write letters of appreciation and encouragement. (Sincerity and vulnerability are needed.)

Ask for volunteers to read their letters. Give students stamped envelopes to address. Tell the group you will mail the letters later.

DEBRIEFING   Say: **What you just wrote may have been difficult for some of you. Telling a parent how much you care for and love him or her may not make your top 10 list of exciting things to do. But just think about the power it will have.**

Those words contain incredible good will. God can bless your message. It can bring hope and healing. It may open new doors for talking and sharing with a parent. Trust God to be part of the process. He leads us in kindness, compassion, and forgiveness.

PRAYER STARTER   Pray that group members will rely on God's help to follow His will, respecting their parents more and more.

···················*Don't forget to mail the letters!*···················

JUMP FOR JOY

MAIN IDEA God desires that we find joy in our lives. Thank and praise Him for His blessings.

SCRIPTURE Psalm 100

SUPPLIES Newsprint and marking pens.

INTRODUCTION Sit in a circle. Ask group members to think of something exciting or happy that has happened to each of them in recent days. One at a time tell them to jump up and shout it out. Ask:

- What can deflate your joy?

- Why is it sometimes hard to find something to be joyful about?

ACTIVITY Say: **The consequences of sin affect our world and our lives. This isn't what God wants for us. God really wants us to experience the joy of living. So He sent Jesus to suffer the consequences of our sin on the cross. Jesus brings us the joy of forgiveness and eternal life. Being thankful and praising God's name are ways we can express our joy in the Lord.**

Divide into groups of three. Give each group a sheet of newsprint and some marking pens. Read each line of Psalm 100 and ask everyone to repeat your words.

Tell the groups to write a six-line psalm of praise modeled after Psalm 100. Share the results by having each group jump up and shout their words of praise.

DEBRIEFING Say: **God gives us so much. Sometimes we forget that each day is full of reasons to praise God. It's important to spend some time each day recognizing our blessings and thanking and praising God for our joys. It's important to spend some time each day alone with Jesus. Knowing that God's love endures forever is just one of many reasons to celebrate.**

PRAYER STARTER Pray that group members will make a daily appointment with God to praise and thank Him for His great love.

FOLLOW THE LEADER

MAIN IDEA   Different people and things demand our attention, but Jesus is the only one who can transform us into whom God wants us to be.

SCRIPTURE   Romans 12:1–2

SUPPLIES   The Dr. Seuss book *Sneetches* (Random House, 1961), green paper, tape, and scissors.

INTRODUCTION   Ask the group whom they most admire or want to be like at this moment. Share responses. Say: **A lot of people and things demand our attention. Sometimes we follow the wrong voices just to be liked. It's hard to know which way to go.**

ACTIVITY   Divide into two groups. Give one group green paper, scissors, and tape. Tell them to cut out large green stars and tape them on their arms. Give the other group green paper, scissors, and tape, but tell them to not do anything with it yet.

Say: **I'm going to read a story by Dr. Seuss called *Sneetches*. You are the two kinds of people represented in the story. Listen carefully and follow along with appropriate actions.** Read the story. Ask:

- Why do you think everyone wanted to be exactly alike?

- Describe a time you were like the Sneetches and did something just so you wouldn't be different.

DEBRIEFING   Read Romans 12:1–2. Ask:

- What do you think Paul is talking about?

- How does this affect your behavior as Christians?

Say: **As Christians, the Holy Spirit helps us respond to Christ's forgiving and saving grace. As we follow Christ, we don't end up in someone else's mold. We can be individuals with our own personalities. Don't conform to the standards of the world. Conform to God's plan in Christ.**

PRAYER STARTER   Pray that God's Spirit will guide and strengthen each of you to stand up and be a Christian example for others.

THE POWER OF KINDNESS

MAIN IDEA   God loves us and helps us share His love by being kind to others.

SCRIPTURE   Ephesians 4:32

SUPPLIES   A small pet—kitten, puppy, hamster, goldfish—that you can keep out of sight until needed.

INTRODUCTION Ask volunteers to complete this statement: "The kindest thing someone could do for me right now is …" Ask:

● When was the last time someone was kind to you?

● How do you feel when you receive an unexpected dose of kindness?

ACTIVITY   Bring out the pet and let the group enjoy it. Point out the gentleness and kindness group members show to the pet. Ask:

● What do you notice about animals when you are kind to them?

● Why do you think people often have a natural inclination to be loving with pets?

DEBRIEFING   Read Ephesians 4:32. Ask:

● What's the ultimate act of kindness God did for us?

● How does the forgiveness Christ won for us on the cross motivate us in dealing with other people?

● When is it difficult for you to forgive someone?

● What effect do you think it would have had on the church in Ephesus if all the members started being kind and compassionate to one another?

● What effect would sharing kindness have in your own home?

Say: **Sometimes it seems easier to care for and be kind to a pet than to show kindness and compassion to our family and friends. Maybe it's because pets just love us and can't talk back! But people, as well as pets, need big doses of kindness.**

God treats us with the highest kindness and compassion possible—He sent His own Son to the cross to win forgiveness and new life for us. God's Holy Spirit gives us the power to share that kindness and compassion with others.

Ask group members to plan specific acts of kindness to do for someone in the coming week. Share the ideas.

PRAYER STARTER Thank God for His great compassion and kindness offered through Jesus. Ask Him to empower each of you with the ability to share His forgiveness and love.

LIGHTEN UP

MAIN IDEA   All of us carry heavy burdens that we can turn over to God and let Him lighten our load.

SCRIPTURE   1 Peter 5:6–7; Matthew 11:28

SUPPLIES   Three hardback books, three sheets of paper, three rubber bands, and a pen for each person. A heavy trash bag or large sack.

INTRODUCTION   Give everyone a pencil and three sheets of paper. On each sheet of paper, have them write down a problem that really bothers them.

Say: **Sometimes we call our problems "heavy burdens." How can a problem feel like a heavy weight?**

ACTIVITY   Give everyone three books and three rubber bands. Have them take one of their sheets of paper and fasten it to a book with a rubber band.

Ask for volunteers to share what they have written. Pass the sack to the person talking. When finished, that person puts his or her books in the sack and carries it around the circle to the next speaker. Continue in this manner. Eventually the sack will get very heavy and difficult to carry. Ask:

- What did you notice happening as we added more and more problems to the sack?
- How many problems do each of you think you can handle at one time?
- Was there a time in your life when you felt your problems were so heavy you couldn't go on?

DEBRIEFING   Read 1 Peter 5:6–7 and Matthew 11:28. Ask:

- What do you think will happen if you try to carry your burdens without God's help?
- What are some ways God helps you carry your burdens?
- How does it make you feel to know that God cares for you?

Say: **Sometimes we think we're strong enough to go it alone. We're determined to get through those tough times when the problems mount up. But eventually we crash. The load gets too heavy, and we need help carrying it.**

Trust God with your burdens. Take your problems and anxieties to the Lord. Don't try to shoulder them all alone. Jesus showed through His death and resurrection that He has the power to deal with the burden of sin and all our other burdens. God wants to help you carry them.

PRAYER STARTER   Pray that God will help each of you to trust and turn your burdens over to Him.

QUIT YOUR BELLYACHING

MAIN IDEA   God's power in our lives leads to contentment and does away with our need to complain about every little thing.

SCRIPTURE   Philippians 2:5, 13–15

SUPPLIES   A roll of adding-machine tape and marking pens for every two people.

INTRODUCTION   Gather in a circle. Ask:

- What one thing do you complain about most?
- Why do you think complaining is so much fun?
- What kind of reaction do you get out of your parent(s) when you complain?
- What kind of complaining really grates on your nerves?

ACTIVITY   Divide into pairs. Give each pair a roll of adding-machine tape and marking pens. Ask them to begin unrolling the paper and writing down all the things they can think of that people complain about.

When the pairs are finished, have the individuals stand back to back. Take each roll of paper and wrap it tightly around the twosome. The pairs shouldn't be able to move. Ask:

- Well, how do you feel wrapped up in your complaints?
- What are some ways your constant complaining can tie you down?
- What effect do you think your complaining has on your friends, teachers, parents, or other adults?

DEBRIEFING   Read Philippians 2:14–15. Tell the groups to break free from their roll of complaints. Help those that can't break the paper. Ask:

- How can we break free from negative attitudes? (Read Philippians 2:13.)
- Through God's forgiving and renewing power, what can our attitude become? (Read Philippians 2:5.)
- What would your life be like if you would shine like stars in a crooked and depraved society?

Say: **Complaining is an addictive behavior. Eventually, we reach the point where all we do is whine and complain. Every little thing we nag to death. What a lousy way to live.**

God wants better for us. God knows that complaining is destructive and comes to no good. It turns others against us and makes our homes very unpleasant places. If you are a complainer, chill for a while. Let God steer your energy into something more productive. Complaining takes the joy out of life and binds us up. Jesus sets us free.

PRAYER STARTER   Pray that God will help each of you understand the destructive power of complaining and the joy we find in Jesus.

WHAT DOES GOD SEE IN US?

MAIN IDEA   Many people judge us on the outside; God cares what is in our heart.

SCRIPTURE   1 Samuel 16:1–13

SUPPLIES   Paper plates, scissors, and marking pens.

INTRODUCTION   Gather in a circle. Ask: **When you see someone different from you, what's your first reaction?**

Say: **Usually, we aren't very kind in our judgments of people who seem different. Looking at appearances can lead to dangerous assumptions.**

ACTIVITY   Give each person a paper plate, marking pen, and scissors. Tell everyone to make masks out of the paper plates by cutting out a place for eyes, nose, and mouth and drawing any other facial features.

Ask everyone to think of three things about themselves that no one knows or ever sees and write them on the back of the mask. Have everyone hold the masks over their faces. Ask:

- Why do we often judge people by outward appearances?

- Why is it sometimes scary to let people see what we're really like?

- Why would you like to keep your three statements hidden? Why might you like to reveal them?

DEBRIEFING   Read 1 Samuel 16:1–13. Ask:

- How do you feel knowing that God never judges you on your physical appearance?

- Why do you think a person's heart is more important to God?

- How do you feel knowing that God knows the real you?

Say: **Everyone in our group is special to God. Each of you has been given talents and spiritual gifts to use for God's kingdom. You see, God looks inside that heart of yours to find the true person. When He looks at the heart of believers, God does not see our sin but our Savior. Through the power of the Holy Spirit, He fills our hearts with faith, compassion, kindness, understanding, good will, and love. These things matter most.**

PRAYER STARTER Pray that God's Spirit will produce loving and caring hearts in all of you.

MOLDING THE CLAY?

MAIN IDEA   God is at work like a potter to shape our lives into beautiful creations of the Master.

SCRIPTURE   Jeremiah 18:1–4; 2 Corinthians 5:17

SUPPLIES   Clay or play dough for each person.

INTRODUCTION   Divide into groups of three or four people. Quietly assign each group a specific emotion, such as anger, frustration, surprise, fear, hatred, or joy. Ask them to depict this emotion in a silent human sculpture. One at a time, let the groups get into their scenes. Ask everyone else to guess the emotion being depicted. Discuss with the group:

● What's hard about trying to convey an emotion without words?

● How were you able to guess what each group represented?

Say: **Our emotions have a lot to do with creating the kind of person we are. Sometimes our emotions even control us.**

ACTIVITY   Give everyone a piece of clay or some play dough. Ask each person to make a symbol that depicts a particular personality trait they think God might want them to have or what kind of person they think God wants them to be. Share the results. Ask:

● What was hard about trying to represent God's plan for you through clay?

● What comes to mind when you think about the possibility that God might be shaping your life in some way?

● What are some ways you want God to shape your life?

DEBRIEFING   Read Jeremiah 18:1–4. Say: **The prophet Jeremiah was given a message from God as he watched the potter work. If an object the potter was working on got flawed, he simply started over.** Ask:

● In what ways is that idea similar to the effect of God's forgiveness on us?

● Where do you think Jesus fits into that plan? (Read 2 Corinthians 5:17.)

● What is our new life in Christ like?

Say: **God truly wants to shape our lives as faithful disciples of Jesus. God never gives up on us even though we might think we are flawed or marred or broken. God is always willing to forgive, renew, and empower us.**

PRAYER STARTER   Pray for God's helping hand to shape each of your lives through Christ.

GOD CREATED EVERYTHING GOOD

MAIN IDEA   God created everything good, and He has given us everything we need for victorious living.

SCRIPTURE   Genesis 1:1–2:3

SUPPLIES   Finger paints and a long strip (10 feet) of heavy white paper.

INTRODUCTION   Divide into small groups. Ask each group to try to list in order, from memory, each thing that was made during the six days of creation. Compare results. Ask:

- When you think about the six days of creation, what comes to mind?

- If you were going to give God some advice about doing it all over again, what would you change?

ACTIVITY   Roll out the paper and place finger paints next to it. Tell the groups to position themselves around the paper. (Use a longer sheet if you have a large group.)

Say: **I'm going to read the creation story from Genesis 1. Divide yourselves into six groups representative of the six days. As I read about that day, use your finger paints to interpret that part of creation.** Read the following sections for each day slowly:

First day:	1:3–5
Second day:	1:6–8
Third day:	1:9–13
Fourth day:	1:14–19
Fifth day:	1:20–23
Sixth day:	1:24–31

Allow the groups time to finish their painting. Discuss their interpretations of each day.

DEBRIEFING   Ask the group if they remember the one thing that was said after each day of creation (verses 10, 18, 21, 25, 31). Ask:

- Why do you think it was important for the biblical writer to repeat that phrase?

- What has happened to the world we live in?

- What is God's desire for the people of the world? (See John 3:16.)

Say: **Absolutely, positively, make no mistake about it—God created everything good. But sin marred God's good and perfect plan of creation. So God created His good and perfect plan of salvation to destroy the power of sin. Creation is God's gift to us. Salvation through Jesus Christ is God's gift to us. Let's praise and thank God each day for His great gifts.**

PRAYER STARTER   Pray that God will help each of you understand the beauty and goodness of creation and salvation.

GET THE WORD OUT

MAIN IDEA   God wants us to get the word out to others that Jesus is the Messiah.

SCRIPTURE   Luke 3:1–16

SUPPLIES   A tape player, microphone attachment, and a blank tape.

INTRODUCTION Take a thumbs up or a thumbs down poll concerning the group's opinion of television evangelists. Talk about the ways a television evangelist gets people to listen and pay attention.

ACTIVITY   Read Luke 3:1–16. Say: **John the Baptist was quite a guy. He had a way of piercing your heart with the message of God. What do you think it would have been like to be there to hear him speak?**

Divide into small groups. Tell each group to imagine giving an eyewitness account of John the Baptist. Use the tape player to record an interview with each group. Ask:

- Some people say this man John is just a crazy lunatic. What's your opinion?

- Some people are very angry at his words. How do you feel?

- What's all this stuff he says about preparing the way for some one greater than he is?

- Repent! Repent! What's he talking about?

Gather together and play back the interviews. Discuss the responses.

DEBRIEFING   Say: **It must have been something to be there with John the Baptist. He had a way of making your heart burn inside if you were a sinner. And everyone was. And everyone is. John wanted to get the word out about Jesus. He was faithful to that calling. John said, "Behold the Lamb of God who takes away the sins of the world." Discuss with the group:**

- How can you get the word out about Jesus?

- Where are places you go and who are people you meet that need to hear about Christ?

- What are ways that you can share the love of Jesus besides using words?

- What will happen if we don't get the word out?

Say: **We are the hands, feet, and voices God has chosen to spread His message. It's hard to do that. We get embarrassed or afraid or forgetful. So much other stuff gets in the way. But we can rely on God's power to help us spread the word.**

PRAYER STARTER Pray that God will make each of you strong in His Word and witness.

LIGHTING THE WAY

MAIN IDEA   Jesus wants us to be a light to others, sharing the Good News God has to give them.

SCRIPTURE   Matthew 5:14–16

SUPPLIES   A candle, matches, and a string of outdoor Christmas-tree lights with large bulbs. Remove the bulbs and put them in a bag.

INTRODUCTION   Sit in a circle and light the candle. Turn out the lights. Say: **As we sit here focusing on the light in the center of our circle, let's think of Jesus. He called Himself the light of the world. What's your life like when you focus on Jesus and place Him at the center of your life?**

ACTIVITY   Turn the lights back on. Pass the Christmas light string around the group so each person has an empty socket in front of him or her. Pass around the bag and ask everyone to take one light and hold it. Sit where you can plug in the end of the light string. Turn out the lights again.

Read Matthew 5:14–16 using the candle's light. Say: **Light is a powerful thing. No matter how dark it is, light pushes back the darkness. God calls each of us to be lights in this world, pushing back the darkness as we share God's message and His love. It's an awesome responsibility, but God is with us. He forgives our failures and gives us the power to live as His people, as lights in this world.**

I want each of you to think about a special talent or gift you think God has given you to use to help others. One at a time I want you to tell what it is. But before someone speaks, I will unplug the cord so that person can add his or her lightbulb to the string. After each person shares a gift, I'll plug the string in again.

As you go through the experience, make sure you unplug the string before each person adds his or her lightbulb. The candle will serve as a backup each time you unplug the string. The effect will be dramatic as the light grows brighter and brighter.

DEBRIEFING   Leave the string plugged in and ask:

⬤   What are some ways people are in the dark today?

⬤   What did you notice as each person shared a talent and added his or her lightbulb to the string?

Say: **There is a lot of darkness out there. People need the light that Jesus can bring. Are you willing to share the light of the Gospel and how Christ has brightened your life? Don't be afraid. God is with you. God never runs out of light or love or power.**

PRAYER STARTER   Pray that God will give each of you the courage to share your light with someone in the coming week.

TURN HATE TO LOVE

MAIN IDEA   Through His death and resurrection, Jesus gives us the example and power to love our enemies.

SCRIPTURE   Matthew 5:43–44

SUPPLIES   Current newspaper or magazine, paper, marking pens, & masking tape.

INTRODUCTION   Look through the newspaper or magazine together and draw "angry," jagged arrows pointing to headlines, stories, and pictures about events motivated by hate. Ask the group to think about, but not name or describe, people whom they dislike or hate. Ask:

- What behavior causes you to dislike or hate someone?
- Why does so much hate exist in our world?
- Is hate a stronger emotion than love? Why do you think so?

ACTIVITY   Give everyone paper and marking pens. Ask them to draw a stick figure to represent a person they dislike or even hate. Tell them not to identify the individual in any way. Tape the pictures to the wall.

Hand out more paper. Ask everyone to write one reason per sheet of paper that explains why they dislike the person. Ask group members to stand in front of the pictures they drew. On *GO*, tell them to crumple their papers and throw the wads at their pictures. Establish a prearranged signal to stop the barrage. Stop the group and gather them together. Ask:

- What were you feeling as you threw those paper wads?
- Was the intensity of your feelings frightening?
- What did this experience teach you about the power of hate?

DEBRIEFING   Read: Matthew 5:43–44. Say: **Sometimes hating someone feels so good and right. Satan can convince us pretty easily that it's all right to hate people who hurt us.** Discuss with the group:

- Do you think Jesus had reason to hate people?
- What hateful things did Jesus' enemies do to Him—both before and at the time of His death?
- What was Jesus' reaction towards those who treated Him badly?
- What are some safe ways to handle angry and hateful feelings?

Say: **Jesus knew all about hate. Jealous church leaders worked overtime to try and undermine His ministry. His own disciples slept and then ran away as He faced the agony of arrest, ridicule, and crucifixion. Jesus faced powerful temptation to hate. But He didn't spit in the face of His persecutors or call legions of angels to kill the soldiers who nailed Him to the cross. Instead, He looked at the people whose sins—along with our sins—sent Him to the cross and said, "Father, forgive them, for they don't know what they do."**

Make sure group members know that if someone is abusing them or treating them unfairly, they can come to you, or another responsible adult, and you will find a way to help. **When you're tempted to dislike people and speak hatefully, ask Jesus to heal your hateful feelings and turn them to love and acceptance as He forgives you.**

PRAYER STARTER   Ask God to heal the hateful feelings present in each person and help each of you share the love and forgiveness won and modeled by Jesus.

A RECIPE FOR GROWTH

MAIN IDEA — The power of Jesus in our lives is like the effect yeast has on bread.

SCRIPTURE — Matthew 13:33

SUPPLIES — A calculator, a bread recipe, and two sets of all the ingredients to follow the recipe. In one set of ingredients, leave out the yeast. Copy the bread recipe but omit any mention of yeast.

Note: This devotion will take longer because you will actually bake the bread. It might work best for a lock-in. Or begin the youth meeting or activity with the first part of the devotion. Conduct the business part of the event while the bread is baking. End with the final part of the devotion.

INTRODUCTION — Ask the group to think about how much of their heart and life belongs to Jesus. Say: **Let's make some calculations. If Jesus is a "Christmas and Easter" thing,** (pull out your calculator and figure) **two out of 365 days is .54 percent. If Jesus is just a "Sunday" thing, that's 52 out of 365 days or 14 percent. Actually, even half-time isn't what God wants.** Ask:

◉ What do you think God wants? (See 2 Chronicles 19:9.)

◉ What can change us from half-hearted to whole-hearted people?

ACTIVITY — Take the group to the kitchen where you have previously set out the supplies to make bread. Split the group between the two sets of ingredients.

Say: **We're going to try our skills at making bread. Go ahead and follow the directions.** Give the bread time to rise and then bake the loaves. When it's done, compare the loaves. Pass around pieces of the loaves to taste.

DEBRIEFING — Read Matthew 13:33. Tell the groups that one of the teams used ingredients that didn't include yeast. Ask:

◉ What are some ways that Jesus might be like the action of yeast in our lives?

◉ What are some ways we can be yeast to others?

Say: **Yeast is powerful. It causes bread to rise and taste good. It affects every part of the bread. Jesus affects every part of our lives. Without Jesus, we would end up lifeless and ruined, like bread without yeast. Jesus wants us to experience life with Him and not apart from Him. Jesus also wants us to be yeast—affecting the lives of people around us by telling them the Gospel message of God's forgiveness and love.**

PRAYER STARTER — Pray that the Holy Spirit will lead each of you to whole-hearted faithfulness as Jesus affects your whole life with His power, forgiveness, and grace.

WATCH WHERE YOU STEP

MAIN IDEA   When our eyes are focused on Jesus, we can be sure we are walking the right path.

SCRIPTURE   Matthew 14:28–33; 1 Peter 2:21, 24

SUPPLIES   A long piece of string or yarn.

INTRODUCTION   Divide into pairs. Tell the pairs to face each other and spend one minute looking at their partners without speaking. Now tell the pairs to sit back to back. Ask:

- What's your partner's hair and eye color?

- Describe the clothes the other person is wearing.

- What kind of jewelry does the person have on?

- Is your partner wearing a watch?

Say: **Sometimes we can keep our eyes on something and not really see it at all. Other times our eyes wander from one thing to another. Staying focused is really difficult.**

ACTIVITY   Read Matthew 14:28–33. Stretch the string across the floor. Ask a volunteer to stand at one end of the string and walk along it to the other end. Ask another volunteer to stand on one end of the string, cover his or her eyes, and walk to the other end. Ask a third volunteer to walk the string to the middle, then cover his or her eyes and walk to the end. Discuss the group's observations.

DEBRIEFING   Why was it easier for some people to walk than others?

- Why do you think Peter had trouble walking?

Say: **Peter was doing great as long as he kept his eyes on Jesus. Then he took his eyes off Christ and paid attention to the wind and the waves around him. He started to sink.**

It was just like trying to walk that string. When our volunteers could focus their eyes on it, they did fine. When they tried to walk it blind, they couldn't always stay on it. Keep your eyes on Jesus every day. He leads you through this life and to eternal life. Peter tells us this very thing in 1 Peter 2:21, 24. Read the Bible verses.

PRAYER STARTER Pray that God's Holy Spirit will keep each of you focused on Jesus.

PUTTING LOVE INTO PRACTICE

MAIN IDEA   We learn about love from the Lord.

SCRIPTURE   Matthew 22:36–40

SUPPLIES   Blank calendar pages and pencils.

INTRODUCTION   Ask the group to spell the word *love.* Now ask them to think of a word or phrase that starts with one of those letters that describes some aspect of love. Share responses.

ACTIVITY   Give each person a blank calendar page and pencil. Read Matthew 22:36–40. Take group members through the following process of writing love goals for each day of the coming month.

1. Write down a specific action for each day of the coming week that would demonstrate love for God.

2. Write down a specific action for each day of the second week that would show love and care for self. (Participants could complete the phrase: "I will be kind to myself by … ")

3. Write down a specific action for each day of the third week that would communicate love to family and friends.

4. Write down a specific action for each day of the fourth week that would show love for neighbors.

Share some of the responses.

DEBRIEFING

● Why do you think Jesus told us to love God with all our heart, soul, and mind?

● What do you think it means to love a neighbor as yourself?

● Why is it sometimes hard to love ourselves?

● Where do you think love begins: loving God, loving others, or loving yourself? Why?

Say: **Talking about love is easy. But when it comes to putting it into practice, we sometimes come up a little short. For the next month you have a daily schedule to help you do something loving. It's going to be a tough challenge. But the power of the Holy Spirit can enable you to do it. You'll find that your life will be very different. Take it one day at a time.**

PRAYER STARTER   Pray that God will empower each of you to follow through on your love commitments.

·········*Check in with the group at the end of each week to see how everyone is doing.*·········

THE HIGH COST OF THE RIGHT STUFF

MAIN IDEA Jesus forgives us even when we make earthly treasures all-important in our lives. He turns our hearts back to Him.

SCRIPTURE Matthew 6:19–21

SUPPLIES Magazines and catalogs with clothing, shoes, CDs, sports equipment, and other items popular with your group. Several sheets of poster board, scissors, and tape or glue.

INTRODUCTION Say: **Dressing the right way and having the right stuff can help us feel good about ourselves.** Ask the group to discuss some popular clothing styles, designer names, popular singing groups, etc.

ACTIVITY Ask the group to look through the magazines and catalogs, cut out everything they'd like to have—price is no object—and glue or tape the pictures on the poster board. Ask the group to look at the things they chose. Discuss:

- Which things do you really long to have?

- How important is it to have the right stuff?

- How are kids who can't afford—or aren't interested in—current styles treated at your school?

- Have you ever felt left out or been ridiculed because you didn't have the right stuff? Tell us about it.

DEBRIEFING Read Matthew 6:19–21. Discuss:

- What does Jesus say will happen to earthly treasures?

- What do you think it means to "store up treasures in heaven"?

- Is it always wrong to want and enjoy material things?

Say: **Jesus reminds us that earthly treasures don't last. God gives us many blessings and invites us to enjoy them. It isn't wrong to want things that you enjoy. Desiring earthly things only becomes sinful when that desire fills our hearts and minds and makes us feel we can't be satisfied or accepted by others without fulfilling it.**

God's Holy Spirit fills us with faith and love for Jesus—our only lasting Treasure. Jesus won a home for us in heaven through His life, death, and resurrection. He is the one who gives us our sense of worth and satisfaction. He is the Treasure that lasts forever.

PRAYER STARTER Ask God to keep your hearts filled with love for your Treasure that lasts forever.

MENDING BROKEN RELATIONSHIPS

MAIN IDEA   God works in our lives to help us mend broken and painful relationships.

SCRIPTURE   Romans 8:28

SUPPLIES   Four glue bottles. Cut out four large red hearts from poster board. Write one of these Bible verses on each heart: Galatians 5:22–23; Ephesians 4:4–5:2; Colossians 3:13; 1 John 4:19. Cut each heart into four puzzle pieces.

INTRODUCTION   Gather in a circle and then break it apart into four sections. Sit down. Ask for reasons why relationships between people sometimes break apart. Say: **All of us have friendships and other relationships that sometimes don't do well and break apart. Kind of like this circle right now.** Share some of the general reasons why the group thinks relationships break apart.

ACTIVITY   Give each section a glue bottle and a heart puzzle. Have them glue the heart pieces together. Say: **Jesus mended our broken relationship with God by obtaining forgiveness for us through His death on the cross. Now Jesus provides the power and the tools to glue together our other broken relationships.**

Have each group read their Bible verse and explain how it can repair relationships.

DEBRIEFING   Read Romans 8:28. Say: **God is always at work in our lives even when we have broken relationships. Paul says that good can come out of bad situations if we trust Jesus to help us get through.** Discuss with the group:

- What good can come from a broken relationship?

- How can Jesus help us fix broken relationships?

- What's the Christian way to break off girl-boy friend relationships?

Say: **Let God help repair broken relationships. He's got the "know-how" and experience. Trying to go it alone won't solve anything. Trust the power of Christ to be at work in you and the other person.**

PRAYER STARTER   Pray that even as God repairs our sinful hearts, He will also repair broken hearts and broken relationships.

BREAKING DOWN THE BARRIER

MAIN IDEA   God promises us that nothing can ever separate us from His love in Jesus Christ.

SCRIPTURE   Romans 8:38–39

SUPPLIES   A cupcake for every person and three large banquet tables.

INTRODUCTION   Ask the group to give you a definition for the word *separation.* Now ask them to think about how many days they think they could be separated from the following people before they really missed them:

parents

brothers/sisters

favorite teachers

best friends

Say: **When we get separated from the people we care about, we begin to feel lonely inside. Separation is hard to handle. It would be especially difficult if we could be separated from God.**

ACTIVITY   Place three tables together. Put all the cupcakes in the middle, out of reach. Place group members around the edge of the tables and ask them to clasp their hands behind their backs. Say: **When I say go, I want you to try and get one of the cupcakes, but you can't use your hands or take your feet off the floor.** (They won't be able to get the cupcakes even though they try.) Discuss with the group: **How do you feel when you can't reach something you want?**

DEBRIEFING   Move the tables so group members can get a cupcake and sit in a circle with you. Read Romans 8:38–39. Say: **Without Jesus, people have experiences with God somewhat like you just had with the cupcakes. God seems just out of reach and there's nothing they can do about it. But Jesus came to restore us to a right relationship with God, and nothing can ever separate us from His love. Through Jesus we can know God in a new and special way. Jesus has removed the barrier of sin through His death and resurrection and makes us His own people.**

PRAYER STARTER   Pray that God will always assure each of you that through Jesus nothing can separate us from His love.

KNOCK! KNOCK!

MAIN IDEA Jesus invites us to confidently pray to our heavenly Father, knowing He will answer us and give us what we need.

SCRIPTURE Matthew 7:7–8

SUPPLIES Paper and marking pens.

INTRODUCTION Give everyone paper and a marking pen. Ask them to draw a picture or describe something they have been asking for recently.

ACTIVITY Before beginning the activity, send one person out to hide in another room in your facility and close the door. Instruct the individual to open the door and ask, "May I help you?" whenever someone knocks.

Say: **I want everyone to fan out inside the building and start knocking on doors. When you find the door where our volunteer is, he or she will open the door and ask, "May I help you?" Go inside and wait quietly for the rest of the group to find you.**

DEBRIEFING Gather with the group in the new room. Read Matthew 7:7–8. Say: **Earlier we talked about things we had been asking for recently. In these verses Jesus invites us to ask our Father for anything we need and to talk with Him about anything that's troubling us.**

How did it feel to keep knocking on doors that didn't open? Sometimes we ask for the wrong things in the wrong places. Jesus reminds us that sinful parents can give their children good gifts. How much more can our heavenly Father give us the help that we need—including opening the door to heaven for us through the sacrifice of His Son. Discuss with the group:

- Is anything too big or too small to bring to God in prayer?

- If we don't get exactly what we ask for, does that mean God isn't listening?

- How does the fact that our heavenly Father is always listening and ready to help make you feel?

PRAYER STARTER Thank God for answering your prayers and giving you your greatest gift—the open door to heaven.

THE GOLDEN RULE

MAIN IDEA   God has definite ideas on how we are to treat others.

SCRIPTURE   Luke 6:31; 1 John 4:7–19

SUPPLIES   Before leading this devotion, select a charitable organization in your city or a needy family that the group will adopt for a set period of time. Newsprint and marking pens.

INTRODUCTION   Ask the group to share some things that people have done to them recently that they didn't particularly like. Ask:

- How do you like to be treated?

- How do you usually treat other people?

- Describe a time when you did something that really hurt someone else.

- Describe a time you were really hurt.

Say: **Sometimes we end up treating people the way they treat us. That's not God's advice on how to handle our relationships with others.**

ACTIVITY   Say: **God doesn't say treat people as they treat you. Listen to His words.** Read Luke 6:31. Tell the group they are going to put that command of Scripture into practice. Discuss the special family you are going to adopt. Make a list of things they need on newsprint. Divide those items among group members. Set a time to meet to deliver the items. Decide as a group how often to deliver supplies.

DEBRIEFING   Say: **Now comes the big question: WHY? Why do we do this? Is it because we have to or because it makes us feel good? The Bible gives us the answer to WHY.**

Read 1 John 4:19. Then slowly read 1 John 4:7–19. Have the group jump for joy every time they hear the word *love* or *loved.*

PRAYER STARTER Pray that God would fill your hearts with His love so that it over-flows in your actions towards others.

REBUILDING

MAIN IDEA   God is there to help us when everything falls apart and we have to start over.

SCRIPTURE   Nehemiah 2:11–13, 17–19; 4:6–9; 6:15–16

SUPPLIES   Arrive early and place everything in your meeting area in a pile in the center of the room. Create an atmosphere of chaos. Don't let anyone in the room.

INTRODUCTION Meet with everyone outside your meeting area. Say: **I have some bad news. Something happened to our room. It's torn apart. It's a mess. All the furniture has been thrown in a big pile.** Open the door and let everyone look into the room.

ACTIVITY   Ask for ideas on how to put the room back together. Decide on a plan and then carefully put everything back where it belongs. Sit in a circle when the room gets back to normal. Ask:

- What was your first reaction when you saw the room?

- Can you describe a time you experienced a disaster and felt like you were starting over?

DEBRIEFING   Say: **There was a time in the history of the Israelites when they had to start all over. They had been forced into captivity and the walls of Jerusalem were destroyed. Finally, they were allowed to go back home. They needed to repair the walls of their city so they could be secure again. Here's how the book of Nehemiah describes what happened.** Read Nehemiah 2:11–13, 17–19; 4:6–9; 6:15–16. Discuss with the group:

- What do you think conditions would have been like back then?

- Would you have been one of the people willing to travel back to your homeland to help rebuild the walls? Why?

- Describe a time you faced the tough job of rebuilding something.

Say: **God was with the Israelites, and they got the wall rebuilt. God is also with you when you have a disaster or tragedy and have to start over again. Rebuilding is hard. It would be impossible without God's love and care and guidance. When you have to begin again somewhere in your life, be sure to let Jesus be a part of that. Jesus has all power—even over sin, death, and the devil. You will get encouragement through Christ that you won't find anywhere else.**

PRAYER STARTER Pray for God's help in facing difficulties in life—whether physical, spiritual, emotional, or relational.

IT ONLY LOOKS IMPOSSIBLE

MAIN IDEA   God helps us through times that seem impossible and gives us the gift of eternal life, possible only through His Son.

SCRIPTURE   Mark 10:27

SUPPLIES   Paper; a trash can; a large, yellow construction-paper star for each person; and marking pens.

INTRODUCTION   Tell the group about a time you faced what you thought was an impossible situation and felt like giving up. Ask group members to share similar situations.

ACTIVITY   Say: **It's easy to give up and quit, especially when we feel things are impossible. On a piece of paper write a phrase, such as "I give up," that you find yourself saying in tough situations. Then crumple your paper into a wad and toss it into the trash can.**

DEBRIEFING   Say: **One day Jesus' disciples asked Him how it was possible for anyone to be saved, especially rich people who are tempted to hang onto earthly riches instead of giving God first place in their hearts. Jesus answered His disciples with the words of Mark 10:27, "With man this is impossible, but not with God; all things are possible with God."** Discuss with the group:

- What do you think Jesus meant by these words?

- How can His words help you in troubled times?

Say: **By dying on the cross for your sins and rising again, Jesus makes it possible for you to be saved and become members of God's kingdom. On our own, we could never be one with God. Knowing that God loves us enough to save us, we are confident that God will help us in every situation, even ones that seem impossible to us.**

Tell everyone to write the words *All things are possible with God* on their stars. Say: **Hang your star in your room this week. Let it remind you to look to God in troubled times.**

PRAYER STARTER   Thank God for accomplishing the seemingly impossible act of saving us from our sin. Ask Him to strengthen each member of the group with the confidence that He will help them in every situation.

SHAPING UP

MAIN IDEA   God wants us to be strong and healthy, physically and spiritually.

SCRIPTURE   1 Corinthians 3:16

SUPPLIES   None.

INTRODUCTION Gather in a circle. Ask everyone to stand on one leg and hold the other one up with their hand. See who can stand the longest. Say: **That was just a little warm-up for the physical fitness test we're taking today. But first I want to ask some questions.**

- How many of you think you can run or jog a mile right now without stopping to rest or walk?

- How many of you think you can do 50 sit-ups without stopping?

- How many of you think you can do 10 push-ups without stopping?

ACTIVITY   Say: **Okay, we're going to have a brief fitness drill. Do the following activities:**

10 jumping jacks
10 sit-ups
10 squat-thrusts

Walk the group around the room to cool down. Return to your circle.

DEBRIEFING   Read 1 Corinthians 3:16. Ask:

- In what ways do you think of yourself as God's temple?

- What are some things that hurt or destroy your body?

- What do you think are some things that might hurt or destroy you spiritually?

- How does it make you feel knowing that God's Spirit is living in you?

Say: **As redeemed people of God, we belong totally to Him. Even our bodies are a gift from God—a gift to be treated with care and used according to God's will. When we're young, we tend to take our bodies for granted. What do you need to do to help keep your body healthy? Get rid of those things that may be doing you harm. Let Jesus help you make some of those tough choices—hear from Him in His Word and talk to Him in prayer. Get rid of stuff that's polluting you physically, spiritually, or emotionally.**

PRAYER STARTER Pray that God will give each of you the courage to take care of the spiritual and physical gifts He gives you.

MATTERS OF THE HEART

MAIN IDEA   God gives us good directions on how Christians can show love.

SCRIPTURE   1 Corinthians 13:4–7

SUPPLIES   A red paper heart and an encyclopedia picture of a heart. Invite a nurse to bring a blood-pressure gauge to your meeting.

INTRODUCTION Say: **The word** *heart* **gets tossed around a lot.** Show the two heart pictures. **"Heart matters" can refer to physical, emotional, or spiritual matters.**

ACTIVITY   Introduce the nurse. Say: **We can check on our heart's physical condition with a simple test. I've invited our guest to take everyone's blood pressure. It's good to have that checked every now and then.**

Go around the group and check everyone's blood pressure. Ask:

- What are some reasons why we might need to have our blood pressure checked?

DEBRIEFING   Ask: **What about the condition of your heart emotionally? As Christians, our heart's emotional response is affected by our heart's spiritual response, which is affected by God's love for us. God first loved us, so we, in turn, show love to others. The Bible tells us about heart matters and about true love.**

Read 1 Corinthians 13:4–7. Ask:

- What do you think is the most important item on that list?

- Which item on that list does your family most need from you right now? Why?

- Which item on that list do your friends most need from you right now? Why?

Say: **God sent Jesus so we would know the true meaning of Christian love. It's the kind of selfless love that gave up everything for us. It's the kind of special love that nothing can ever destroy or harm or eliminate. It's the kind of love we often fail to show to others. But Jesus, because of His love, forgives us and then helps us grow in love. The Holy Spirit, working through the Word and Sacraments, can give us the power and strength to show and live in Christian love, following Christ's example.**

PRAYER STARTER Pray that God will enable each of you to be strong and faithful in matters of the heart.

PROTECTED

MAIN IDEA   God provides us with the armor needed to protect us from evil.

SCRIPTURE   Ephesians 6:11–17

SUPPLIES   Newsprint, construction paper, cardboard, masking tape, scissors, marking pen, and yarn.

INTRODUCTION Ask the group to decide on six things they would need to protect themselves in a war. List them on newsprint. Ask:

● What do you think would really keep you safe?

ACTIVITY   Ask for a volunteer from the group. Stand this person in the center of the group. Set out the newsprint, tape, scissors, yarn, cardboard, and construction paper.

Read Ephesians 6:13–17. Tell the group to dress your volunteer with all the armor mentioned in the passage (belt of truth, breastplate of righteousness, feet fitted with peace, shield of faith, helmet of salvation, sword of the Spirit). Let them be creative in the designs they want to use.

DEBRIEFING: ● How do you feel about the armor you made?

● How effective do you think it would be in a battle?

● Do you know who the enemy is? (Read Ephesians 6:11–12.)

● What do you think is the worst kind of evil facing Christians?

● How is God's armor the strongest of all?

Say: **Every day we feel like we're in a battle zone. There's a lot of bad stuff going on around us. When we know by faith that we're wearing God's armor, we can be courageous and do battle for what's right and good. Remember that Jesus has won the victory over sin and death and He has the power to help us in our daily struggles. Wearing God's armor, the power of the Holy Spirit will give you strength to stand up for Jesus.**

PRAYER STARTER Pray that God's armor will protect each of you in your daily struggles, in Jesus' name.

ROYALTY

MAIN IDEA	God has chosen us through Jesus to be part of His royal priesthood of believers.
SCRIPTURE	1 Peter 2:9–10
SUPPLIES	Construction paper, scissors, and glue or tape.
INTRODUCTION	Say: **There used to be a TV program called "Queen for a Day." Someone would win the right to be treated royally for 24 hours. Imagine that you had just been chosen king or queen for a day. What decrees would you make? What would you do to pamper yourself?** Share responses.
ACTIVITY	Spread out the supplies and ask students to make crowns for themselves. They may design the crowns as elaborately as they want, but they can only use the materials you have provided.
DEBRIEFING	Read 1 Peter 2:9–10. Ask:

● What does it mean when it says we are a royal priesthood?

● What kind of crown do we receive? (Read Revelation 2:10b.)

● As people who have received God's mercy through Jesus, what is our response?

Say: **It's hard for us to think of ourselves as royalty. This is nothing we deserve. We receive it because we have been made people of God through Christ's death and resurrection. We are part of that royal priesthood of believers who share a common Lord and Savior. We have been given the title of holy because our sins are forgiven and we belong to God. Let's share that important Gospel message with everyone we meet so that they also can inherit the crown of eternal life through Jesus.**

PRAYER STARTER Pray that God's royalty and holiness will be a part of your hearts and lives always.

LITTLE LIES NEVER HURT

MAIN IDEA   Our true and faithful God desires that honesty follow us every-where.

SCRIPTURE   Colossians 3:9

SUPPLIES   A thesaurus.

INTRODUCTION   Say: **Lies cover up the truth. Sometimes we even cover up a lie by calling it something else. What other names do we use for lies?** (Exaggerations, fibs, fabrications, white lies, half-truths—check the thesaurus for other possibilities.)

ACTIVITY   Sit in a circle. Tell group members to think of two statements about themselves that no one else in the group would know. The only catch is that one statement is the truth and the other is a lie. The object of the game is to see if other group members can decide which one is the lie.

Go around the circle one at a time and identify the statement that's a lie. Each group member who chooses the correct statement gets 10 points. After everyone shares their statements, see who has the most points.

DEBRIEFING   Read Colossians 3:9. Ask:

- Why do you think it's often so easy to fool people with a lie about yourself?

- What are some consequences of lying?

- What happens to your relationships if you lie or someone lies to you?

Say: **Being a disciple of Christ starts getting hard when we have to face up to those little lies. We don't think they hurt anything. Nobody will know. Nobody will find out. They're just harmless, little fibs. But God knows and God grieves every time we lie to each other. No matter what we may call it, the bottom line is that a lie is a sin. Actually, the bottom line is that we are sinners who need our Savior's forgiveness.**

We need our Savior's transforming power to fight the temptation to sin. The next time you are tempted to lie about something, think about your friend Jesus standing there beside you. Rely on Him to give you the courage to tell the truth.

PRAYER STARTER   Pray that God will grant each of you the strength to say no to lies and to become people of truth.

WORDS THAT HURT

MAIN IDEA Words can hurt people and leave deep scars. Jesus leads us to forgive and show kindness.

SCRIPTURE Ephesians 4:29, 32

SUPPLIES Plastic pill bottles, marking pens, masking tape, slips of paper, and pencils.

INTRODUCTION Shout: **Sticks and stones may break my bones, but words will never hurt me.** Then ask the group what's wrong with that old cliché.

ACTIVITY Give each person an empty pill bottle, a piece of tape, a marking pen, slips of paper, and a pencil.

Say: **Think about the mean words or phrases people use. Some of them may have hurt you while others may have hurt someone else. Write each of them on a separate slip of paper. Roll them up and put them in the pill bottle. If you're including an obscene word or statement, just use the first letter of the word and dashes for the other letters.**

Tell each person to write the word *Poison* on a strip of tape and wrap it around the bottle. Ask:

● How does bad language poison our attitudes?

● How does hurtful language poison our relationships?

DEBRIEFING Read Ephesians 4:29. Ask:

● How do you feel when someone blows you away with hurtful language?

● How do you think God feels about all these ugly words and phrases?

Say: **We live in a time when ugly words seem to be the "in" thing. What is the antidote to this kind of poison?** The last verse of Ephesians 4 tells us. Read verse 32. **Jesus forgives us and helps us, leading us to forgive and help others.**

As Christians, led by the Lord, we can talk in such a way that builds people up instead of tearing them down. You can have a tremendous influence on changing the language of your peers. Ask the group to give examples of the kinds of things they can say to build someone up.

PRAYER STARTER Pray that God will lead each of you to use beautiful building-up words, not ugly tearing-down words.

HEADLINE NEWS

MAIN IDEA   Jesus is the same yesterday, today, and forever.

SCRIPTURE   Hebrews 13:8

SUPPLIES   Paper, marking pens, Bibles, and several newspapers.

INTRODUCTION   Display newspapers. Ask the group to share ideas about the kinds of stories that always seem to make headline news in a newspaper or on the TV and radio. Share responses.

ACTIVITY   Give each person a Bible, paper, and a marker. Tell them to skim through the gospels of Matthew, Mark, Luke, or John. Say: **Pick a story from Jesus' life that you think would have made headline news. Title the story and write a brief summary as it would appear today in a newspaper or on the TV news.** Share the stories.

DEBRIEFING   Read Hebrews 13:8. Ask:

● What were you thinking as you wrote your own news story?

● How do you think people today would react to your article?

● Why is it important to see Jesus as the same yesterday, today, and forever?

● How can that strengthen your faith?

Say: **The same Jesus that walked in Judea is here walking with us right now. He will also be with us tomorrow. What He said would save the people back then is the same thing that He says will save us today. That saving power will not change tomorrow either.**

Jesus never goes away, never abandons us, and never leaves us alone. He was there for His disciples and those who believed in Him. He is here, just as real now as then. Through the power of the Holy Spirit, we are saved by faith. Our Savior is alive and with us. Easter morning happens every day.

PRAYER STARTER Pray that God's Holy Spirit will make Jesus a real power and presence for each of you each day.

FAULT FINDERS

MAIN IDEA   Jesus tells us to pay attention to our own faults and not judge others. He offers forgiveness for the times we ignore our sins and condemn others.

SCRIPTURE   Matthew 7:1–5

SUPPLIES   Craft sticks (tongue-depressor size) or strips of balsa wood from a craft store, marking pens, and twine or a glue gun.

INTRODUCTION   Talk to the group about the faults of some well-known figure who's receiving a lot of negative media attention at the moment. Ask the group to do some fault-finding of their own about that individual.

ACTIVITY   Hand everyone a strip of wood and ask them to use a marking pen to draw a pair of eyes on it. Pair off the group and have each twosome cover their eyes with the wood. As they "look" at each other through the wood, have them jokingly list each other's faults. Then call the group back together.

DEBRIEFING   Read Matthew 7:1–5. Say: **It's pretty easy—and kind of fun—to judge others, isn't it?** Ask:

● Could you see your partner clearly when you held the wood over your eyes?

● What stern warning does Jesus give us about judging others?

Say: **We are often blinded by our own sin and overly concerned about the sins of others. Jesus tells us to be concerned about the "plank" of our own sin before we worry about a speck of sin in anyone else.**

Have each pair tie or glue their sticks together to make a cross. Place all the crosses in the center of the group. Say: **God freely forgives our sins because His Son paid for them on the cross. When God's Holy Spirit convicts us of the fact that we are forgiven sinners, it's easier for us to help others acknowledge their sins and find positive ways to help them.**

Looking at the crosses, let's each confess our own faults silently and ask God's help in forgiving others as He forgives us.

PRAYER STARTER   Ask God's forgiveness for your sin of fault-finding. Ask Him to show you how to relate to others in a way that shares His love rather than points out their faults.

WISE ADVICE

MAIN IDEA   God provides people in our lives who can give us good advice and help us learn that Jesus bears all our burdens with us and makes them lighter.

SCRIPTURE   Exodus 18:13–26; Matthew 11:28

SUPPLIES   Newsprint, masking tape, and marking pens.

INTRODUCTION   Tape sheets of newsprint on the walls of the room. Ask group members to think about the best advice they have ever been given. Tell them to sum up the advice in one sentence and write it on one of the sheets of newsprint.

ACTIVITY   Ask a volunteer to sit in a chair in the center of the group. Say: **Our volunteer will serve as our great source of wisdom and advice today. Think of something—nothing silly—that teens really need help handling and ask our sage's advice.**

Ask group members to seek advice, one-on-one, seated in front of the sage. After three or four persons have received advice, ask a new volunteer to be the sage. At the close of the activity ask:

- How did you feel about the advice you got?
- Was it easier to ask for advice or give it?
- At what times in your lives do you really wish you had someone whom you could trust to go to for advice?

DEBRIEFING   Read Exodus 18:13–26. Say: **Moses had been trying to handle the burden of declaring God's will to the Israelites and giving them advice all by himself. Moses' father-in-law told him, "The work is too heavy for you; you cannot handle it alone." Jethro suggested Moses choose capable men to handle simple problems and handle only the difficult cases himself.**

Jesus gives us similar advice. Read Matthew 11:28. **He says He will share our burdens and give us rest. Jesus invites us to bring every problem and decision to Him. He promises to give us the best advice through His Word and to bear our burdens with us—to the point of bearing our burden of sin on the cross.**

Jesus also surrounds us with people who can give us Christian advice and help us with our problems. Ask:

- Who are some of the people to whom you can go for advice?
- What can you do in situations that seem hopeless and times when you're afraid to go to someone for help? (Be alert for group members who hint at problems they are struggling with alone. Quietly offer to speak with them privately.)

PRAYER STARTER   List names of people who can give group members sound Christian advice and thank God for them.

GOD'S REQUIREMENTS

MAIN IDEA   In Jesus, God gives us the example and the ability to meet His requirements for Christian living.

SCRIPTURE   Micah 6:8

SUPPLIES   Newsprint and marking pens.

INTRODUCTION   Divide into groups of three. Give each group newsprint and a marking pen. Ask each group to make a list of 10 important requirements a high school senior should meet to prepare for a successful future. Compare lists when finished.

ACTIVITY   Divide the group in half. Each group will start a new church and make requirements for membership.

Group 1 will form "This Is the Law Church" and establish strict requirements that members must meet exactly.

Group 2 will form "Love of Jesus Church" and establish requirements for members that model Jesus' love and example for us.

Let each group present their requirements when finished. Ask:

  Which church would you be most likely to join? Why?

  What requirements do we follow to become a member at our church?

  What do you think God's requirements are for being a Christian?

DEBRIEFING   Read Micah 6:8. Say: **Just before this verse, God's children have asked what they can give to God to meet His requirements and receive His forgiveness. Should they make burnt offerings, bring thousands of rams, sacrifice their firstborn children? In the verse we just read, Micah answers that none of these things is necessary. God requires that we act justly, love mercy, and walk humbly with Him.**

Those requirements may sound easy compared to offering a child as a sacrifice, but they are only possible for us because God offered His Son as a sacrifice. God justly forgives our sins because Jesus lived a perfect life and took our punishment upon Himself. We love mercy because it is God's mercy that saves us. We walk humbly as God's Holy Spirit gives us the faith and power to walk with Jesus. Discuss with the group:

  How will God's requirements—act justly, love mercy, and walk humbly with Him—guide us as we deal with our family? our friends?

PRAYER STARTER Thank God for giving you His Son to satisfy the requirements of the Law and ask His Holy Spirit's blessing to keep you walking humbly with Him.

SPRING SOUL-CLEANING

MAIN IDEA   God washes us clean of sin through the water and Word of Baptism and the sacrifice of His Son.

SCRIPTURE   Mark 1:1–5

SUPPLIES   Poster board, hole punch, string, and marking pens.

INTRODUCTION   Ask group members what they might do to prepare if they knew for certain that Jesus was returning the next day.

ACTIVITY   Divide into small groups. Ask each group to make a sandwich board by punching holes in the top corners of two pieces of poster board and tying them together. On their signs they should write messages such as "Repent! The kingdom of heaven is at hand!" Have each group—one person wearing the group's sign—give a short exhortation, calling for repentance.

DEBRIEFING   Gather in the sanctuary by your baptismal font. Say: **At the time Jesus began His public ministry, His cousin, John the Baptist, was calling for people to repent, much as you did.** Read Mark 1:1–5. **John preached a baptism of repentance. He called the people to completely turn from their sin and be baptized.**

At the baptismal font, we received complete forgiveness of sin, thanks to Jesus' living, dying, and rising again for us. The Holy Spirit worked faith in our hearts, giving us the strength to turn away from sin and live as God's children. As Satan continually tries to swim past that baptismal water and pull us into sin again, God gives us the strength to fight temptation and forgives us, because of Jesus, when we give in.

Take turns dipping your hands into the water at the font. Thank God for forgiving your sins. Ask His Spirit's blessing in keeping your faith strong. You may want to invite your pastor to take part in this baptismal remembrance with you.

PRAYER STARTER Thank God for the blessing of Baptism and ask Him for renewed strength in turning away from sin.

HOW TO SUCCEED IN LIFE

MAIN IDEA   God's advice for Joshua's success is meant for us too.

SCRIPTURE   Joshua 1:1–9

SUPPLIES   Newsprint, marking pens, and play money.

INTRODUCTION Write *Rich and Famous* on a sheet of newsprint. Ask the group to list words or phrases that indicate you are successful from society's viewpoint.

ACTIVITY   Divide into two groups. Give one group $100,000 in play money. Give the other group no money. Tell both groups to devise a five-part plan that would lead to a successful life starting with the financial resources they were given. Share the results.

DEBRIEFING   Read Joshua 1:1–9. Say: **Joshua was chosen by God to lead the people into the Promised Land after the death of Moses. God gave Joshua the keys to success.** Ask:

● Why do you think God told Joshua to be strong and courageous? Why three times?

● God said He would be with Joshua. If you had been Joshua, what other guarantees of success would you have wanted from God?

● How do you think God is at work in your life right now to help you be successful?

Say: **God's advice for success was simple and straight forward. God told Joshua to be strong and courageous. But Joshua didn't have to rely on himself. He relied on the promise of God (verse 6). He relied on the Word of God (verse 8). And he relied on the powerful presence of God (verse 9).**

You too can be sure that Jesus is with you at every moment. Rely on that and you will find success. Of course, it may never be measured in worldly wealth, but your success will be measured with great happiness.

PRAYER STARTER Pray that God will help each of you understand success from a Christian standpoint and not from the world's view.

SOARING WITH EAGLES

MAIN IDEA   When we feel weary, we are promised God's power, which will carry us on the strength of eagle's wings.

SCRIPTURE   Isaiah 40:28–31

SUPPLIES   None.

INTRODUCTION   Ask the group to think about things in their lives that make them weary—the daily stuff that just drags them down and makes them feel like they can't go on. Each time a volunteer shares something, have the group respond in a mumbling tone, "Weary, weary, weary, weary."

ACTIVITY   Divide into partners of fairly equal height and weight. Tell one partner to get on the floor on their hands and knees. Tell the other person to sit on them. Switch places when the person on the bottom grows tired. See who can support someone the longest. Ask:

- What were you thinking as you started to get tired?

- Describe some other times in your life when you grow weary of carrying burdens.

DEBRIEFING   Read each verse of Isaiah 40:28–31 a line at a time. Have the group repeat each line back to you. Ask:

- Why do you think God never grows tired or weary?

- In what ways do you see God giving strength and power to weak and weary people?

- Why is hope something that renews our strength?

- What do you think it would be like to be an eagle?

Say: **When we grow weary with life, people, or family members, God knows. God knows there are days when we struggle to get through. God knows the pain and anguish we carry. That's why our hope is in Christ. He has power over all things, even power over sin and death. He can empower us to soar above the stuff and junk of life that tries to drag us down. With Jesus we climb higher and higher into the heavens where only eagles soar. Be an eagle.**

PRAYER STARTER   Pray that God will give each of you eagle's wings to soar on the hope and joy only Jesus gives.

DON'T CHICKEN OUT

MAIN IDEA	There are times we must stand up and be counted as believers. God is with us, enabling us to stand tall.
SCRIPTURE	Daniel 6
SUPPLIES	None.
INTRODUCTION	Ask group members which of the following things they would be willing to do:

Rush into a burning building to save a child.

Pull someone from a burning car that's about to explode.

Climb a high ladder to save an animal.

Jump into a flooded stream to rescue a family member.

Step between two people having a fistfight.

Say: **There are times in life when we're faced with challenges. Sometimes we respond and sometimes we don't.**

ACTIVITY	Read Daniel 6 carefully. Appoint members of the group to be cast members of a play to enact this chapter. (Characters include: King Darius, administrators/satraps, Daniel, prison guards, lions, and an angel.) Read each verse of Daniel 6 again and have the characters act out the action.
DEBRIEFING	Gather together and ask:

- What are some reasons Daniel didn't follow the king's decree?
- Describe a time when someone laughed at you because of your faith.
- Think of a time you chickened out because standing up for your faith was too hard for you. Who can you rely on for forgiveness?
- Describe a time in your life when you stood up for what you believed. Thank God for His power that He works in your life.

Say: **Daniel had the courage to defy the king's command because of his unwavering faith in God. Daniel was even willing to risk death in a lions' den before allowing a king's decree to keep him from his daily conversations with God. He trusted the faithfulness and wisdom of God.**

It's easy being a Christian if there's little risk. But some day you may be in a situation where you have to choose between standing up for Christ or chickening out. We can't deal with this through our own power—we must and certainly can rely on the power of God. He will be with you—let Him take charge. Through prayer, Bible study, and meditation on His Word, discover God in your life. Let Jesus be a powerful, daily presence.

PRAYER STARTER Pray that God will help each of you have courage when you face your own lions' den experiences.

CONTROLLING PRIDE

MAIN IDEA   Too much pride can be a temptation to false security.

SCRIPTURE   Matthew 6:1; Colossians 3:17, 23

SUPPLIES   Marking pens, construction paper, and tape.

INTRODUCTION   Ask group members to think about things they have accomplished in their lives. This should include awards they have been given, skills they have developed, goals met, kindnesses shared, etc. Have everyone list their accomplishments on sheets of construction paper. Say: **All of you can be very proud of what you have accomplished.**

ACTIVITY   Ask for a volunteer to stand in the center of the group. Have everyone tape their sheets of construction paper to the volunteer. After all the accomplishments are hung on the human statue, put a sign on him or her that reads *Our Tower of Pride.*

DEBRIEFING   Read Matthew 6:1. Ask:

- After hearing Jesus' advice, what do you think about our Tower of Pride?

- How can our pride hurt others?

- What's dangerous about parading our accomplishments in the face of others?

Say: **Jesus wants us to celebrate our accomplishments and to feel joy in our successes. But this can become a problem if we begin to think we are better than others, if we become self-serving, or if we fail to recognize God's power and blessings in our lives. When we're flashing our good deeds before others, we're heading for trouble.** Read Colossians 3:17, 23. Say: **This Bible passage can guide our attitude toward accomplishments as we replace pumped-up pride with glory to God.**

PRAYER STARTER Pray that God will help each of you have a humble spirit.

WHO IS JESUS?

MAIN IDEA   Consider how you respond to the same question Jesus asked the disciples: "Who do you say that I am?"

SCRIPTURE   Matthew 16:13–18

SUPPLIES   A driver's license, paper, marking pens, and tape.

INTRODUCTION   Ask the group:

● Who am I?

● Who are you?

Take out your driver's license and ask other group members to do the same if they have one with them. Say: **My driver's license tells my name, my license number, and shows what I look like. But it doesn't really tell who I am. I'm more than a name, a number, and a face.**

ACTIVITY   Say: **Now I want to know who Jesus is. We have names for Him. Many artists have drawn pictures of what He could have looked like. But I want to know more. I ask you, who do you say Jesus is?**

Give everyone paper, marking pens, and tape. Tell them to complete this statement: "Jesus, You are … " As they finish tell the group to tape the sheets to the door frame around the entrance to your meeting area. Ask each person to share his or her statement. Ask:

● Why did you choose to describe Jesus in that way?

● Why do you think it's important that each of us be able to state who Jesus is?

DEBRIEFING   Read Matthew 16:13–18. Ask:

● Why didn't some of the people realize Jesus' true identity?

● Peter's statement identified Jesus as true God and the promised Messiah. Why was that important?

● Why can we call Peter's statement a "confession of faith?" (As a group, repeat Peter's words in verse 16.)

Say: **We know a lot of facts about Jesus, but do we know Him? Do you know Him as your personal Lord and Savior? Truly knowing someone involves a relationship. Jesus reaches out to you with His forgiveness, love, care, and friendship. At the end of our time together today, you will walk through this doorway covered with statements about Jesus. Be ready to go to your school and family and live what you believe.**

PRAYER STARTER   Praise God that He is your Lord and Savior and Friend.

WAKE UP!

MAIN IDEA	Just like the disciples, we are often weak and undependable and need our Savior's help.
SCRIPTURE	Matthew 26:36–46
SUPPLIES	Newsprint and marking pens.
INTRODUCTION	Ask the group to tell you things that bore them and put them to sleep. Ask: **What was the worst experience you ever had when you fell asleep somewhere you shouldn't have?** See who can come up with the best "snoozed" story.
ACTIVITY	Divide into two teams. Give each team a sheet of newsprint and marking pen. Tell them to create—ala David Letterman—the top 10 times they should never fall asleep. For example, one item might say "Never fall asleep in the middle of a speech—when you are the speaker." Hang up the lists and share them.
DEBRIEFING	Read Matthew 26:36–46. Tell the group this scene took place on Maundy Thursday, just after the disciples and Jesus shared the Last Supper. Ask:

- How do you think Jesus felt finding His dearest friends asleep?

- How do you think the disciples felt when Jesus found them "asleep on the job"?

Say: **That last night in the Garden of Gethsemane was horrible for Jesus. He needed the support of His disciples, but they fell asleep. It's not that different now. Jesus needs you—your hands, arms, legs, feet, voice, ears, mind, and heart—to share His message and love with others. Sometimes we get bored and fall asleep on the job. We're just like the disciples that Maundy Thursday night. But just like the disciples, we can ask Jesus for forgiveness and the Holy Spirit for His strengthening power.**

PRAYER STARTER Praise God that He helps us in our weakness. Pray that He will lead us to grow in faith and to follow His will.

HOT LINE TO GOD

MAIN IDEA   Prayer is our hot line to God, and we never get a busy signal.

SCRIPTURE   Matthew 6:5–13

SUPPLIES   Index cards, pencils, newsprint, and marking pens.

INTRODUCTION   Give everyone an index card and a pencil. Ask them to write down the three telephone numbers they call most often. Beside each number, have them write the reason they usually call that number. Share responses.

Say: **All of us have people we like to talk to on the phone. You just shared who you call the most. Even God says "call upon Me"** (see Psalm 50:15).

ACTIVITY   Divide into groups of three. Give each group a sheet of newsprint and a marking pen. Tell the groups they have been chosen as the creative teams to develop a new ad campaign for God. God has just installed a new 800 number to call heaven. The teams are to design advertising to get the word out. The ad should increase customer response.

Share results. Take a group vote on the most creative ad. Ask:

- Why would God want an 800 number anyway?
- How effective do you think your ad would be?

DEBRIEFING   Read Matthew 6:5–13. Ask:

- How is prayer like an 800 number to God?

- Why do you think Jesus gave us this model for prayer?

- What do you think Jesus means when He tells us to go into our room and shut the door before we pray?

- What does it mean to babble during a prayer?

- What are some reasons you go to God in prayer?

Say: **Prayer is our hot line to God. Jesus wants us to reach out and bring everything going on in our lives to Him. Jesus said He will be right there to take our requests. It's promised. It's a done deal. He hears our prayers. He answers them in the way that's best and at the right time. If you need to rediscover this in your life, start today. Call on the Lord—there's never a busy signal.**

PRAYER STARTER   Pray that God will remind each of you of the importance of daily contact with Him.

IT'S NOT FAIR!

MAIN IDEA   God says that revenge is His and calls on us to follow Jesus' example in doing good to those who harm us.

SCRIPTURE   Matthew 5:38–42

SUPPLIES   Paper and pens.

INTRODUCTION   Say: **A discipline technique called "natural consequences" is popular right now. A teen who drives carelessly and gets involved in an accident may have car privileges revoked until he or she can earn the money to pay the extra insurance premium.** Ask group members to share experiences they have had dealing with natural consequences.

ACTIVITY   Divide into groups of three. Give each group paper and a pen. Ask the groups to brainstorm outlandish "natural" consequences for teens who break the rules. A teen who arrives home late may have to sleep in the backyard. A student who leaves a book report at home may have to do reports on the "100 Greatest Works of American Literature." After the small groups have had a few minutes to work, come together and share responses.

DEBRIEFING   Say: **In Old Testament times, God gave His people so-called laws of retaliation. These laws could carry natural consequences to the extreme. People who were seriously hurt by others could retaliate in kind—an eye for an eye, a tooth for a tooth, etc. But Jesus corrected our understanding of those laws and gave us His example to follow.** Read Matthew 5:38–42. Ask:

- How easy would it be to let someone who has hurt you, hurt you again?

- Is Jesus telling us in these verses to be wimps?

- How could "going the extra mile" with someone change his or her attitude towards you?

Say: **We all bear the consequences of sin—sickness, unhappiness, loneliness, and more. But thankfully, we don't have to bear the punishment of sin. Jesus did that for us on the cross. That sacrificial love makes it possible for us to treat those who hurt us with forgiveness, as Jesus did. As God's children, the natural consequences we hand out to those who treat us badly should be living examples of Jesus' love and forgiveness.**

PRAYER STARTER   Ask God's blessing to be able to say no to revenge and yes to those who need your help and forgiveness.

EXCUSES, EXCUSES, EXCUSES

MAIN IDEA Our weakness leads us to make lots of excuses; God's strengthening power leads us to respond in faith.

SCRIPTURE Exodus 3:1–14; 4:1–17

SUPPLIES Newsprint, marking pens, and construction paper.

INTRODUCTION Say: **There's something in each of us that tempts us to make excuses instead of owning up to the truth. When excuses work, we think we can make them bigger and bigger and bigger.** Ask group members to describe times excuses backfired on them.

ACTIVITY Divide into two groups. Give one group construction paper and marking pens. Tell them to write down 10 unpleasant things they might be asked to do. (Write each on a separate sheet of paper.)

Give the other group marking pens and construction paper and take them outside your meeting area into the hall. Tell them to write down the 10 best excuses they can think of to avoid an unpleasant situation. (Write each on a separate sheet of paper.)

Shut the door to the meeting area. When the groups have their 10 items completed, tell the group with the problem situations to slide one paper under the door. The group with the excuses should respond by sliding an excuse under the door. (Each group should read the other group's notes. Continue this procedure with the remaining papers.)

When all the answers have been given, gather together and ask:

- What was difficult about communicating with one another under the door?

- What usually happens when we try to get away with something by making an excuse?

DEBRIEFING Gather in a circle. Say: **Moses tried a lot of excuses too—with God.** Read Exodus 3:1–14; 4:1–17. Ask:

- How did God deal with all the excuses Moses had?

- How do think God deals with your excuses?

Say: **It's so easy to give an excuse. We get so good at it. We offer excuse after excuse for not following God's will. Jesus wants us to come to Him, not with excuses but with repentance. He offers us forgiveness, faith, and strength—the same gifts He gave to Moses.**

PRAYER STARTER Pray that God will help each of you face situations directly rather than make excuses.

REBELLION OR OBEDIENCE

MAIN IDEA By nature (sinful nature), we often rebel against rules and commands. Jesus calls us to repentance and brings forgiveness and renewal.

SCRIPTURE Genesis 2:15–17; 3:1–13

SUPPLIES Name tags, paper, and marking pens.

INTRODUCTION Say: **Imagine that you were appointed principal of your school. You have been asked to come up with one rule, and only one rule, for the school. This isn't going to be as easy as it sounds. Making good rules is hard.** Discuss ideas for a single, good rule.

ACTIVITY Give each person a name tag that says *Master*, paper, and marking pens. Say: **Now imagine that you are a boss or master. Write down a list of five commands to give to your servant.** When they are finished, give each person a name tag that says *Servant*. Say: **Now look at your list of commands from the viewpoint of a servant. Ask:**

● How did you like making the commands?

● How did you feel when the roles were reversed?

DEBRIEFING Read Genesis 2:15–17 and 3:1–13. Ask:

● Why do you think God had only that one rule for Adam and Eve?

● What started Eve thinking about breaking that rule?

● What was the result when Adam and Eve decided to rebel against God's rules?

Say: **This story is about each one of us. There's only one rule maker in life and that's God. The Bible tells us about that one main rule to follow in Luke 10:27, "Love the Lord your God with all your heart and with all your soul and with all your strength and with all your mind."**

But this is one rule we break time and again. So God also gives us one Savior, Jesus, who calls us to repentance and to a new life as His people. What is life like when we live as His people?

PRAYER STARTER Pray that Jesus will lead you to follow His ways and His will.

WRAPPED UP IN FEAR

MAIN IDEA   God is always there when we have nowhere else to turn for help and support.

SCRIPTURE   Psalm 46

SUPPLIES   Shelf paper or adding-machine tape (enough to stretch around your meeting room), grocery sacks, and marking pens.

INTRODUCTION   In advance, repeatedly write the word *fear* on a strip of shelf paper or adding-machine tape. The paper should stretch around your meeting room.

Have volunteers help hold the strip of paper so that it surrounds your group. Say: **Because of sin and evil in this world, we're surrounded by many fears. Fear is always with us. Sometimes it's so powerful we can't go on. We feel like there's nowhere else to turn for help and support.**

ACTIVITY   Give everyone a grocery sack and marking pen. Tell them to write on the sack, covering it with all the things they have ever been afraid of in their lifetime. Remind them to think back to all those little kid fears too. (They may choose to draw symbols instead of using words.) Sit together and discuss fear.

Say: **I want everyone to stand up and put your sack over your head so you can't see anything around you. Stretch out your arms as protection. Slowly walk around the room being careful not to bump into someone.** Gather together. Ask:

- What were you thinking during that activity?

- Describe a time when you were so afraid you felt like you were walking blind.

DEBRIEFING   Read Psalm 46 one line at a time. Ask the group to repeat it. Ask:

- In what ways might that psalm help us with our fears?

- How can God be our help in times of trouble?

- How do you feel after hearing the statement that the Lord Almighty is with us?

Say: **Sometimes we feel so fearful and alone that we have no place and no one to turn to. Some people end up drinking, doing drugs, in gangs, or even committing suicide. They feel helpless. God grieves when we get to that point. He calls us to repentance; He calls us to faith.**

Jesus has power to help us with our worst problems—even sin and death. With the psalmist, we ask Him to save us from our fear and our loneliness. "God is our refuge and strength." The psalm is true. God's Word is true.

PRAYER STARTER   Pray that God will assure each of you of His presence and the hope of eternal life with Him.

GOD GETS MAD?

MAIN IDEA The book of Proverbs tells us that there are seven things that really get God angry.

SCRIPTURE Proverbs 6:16–19

SUPPLIES Newsprint, marking pens, and Bibles.

INTRODUCTION Ask the group to think about all the words of wisdom they have been given over the years. What sayings have they heard that they now believe to be true? (These would be things such as "Do to others as you want them to do to you.") Share responses.

Say: **There are many sayings that we discover through life to be wonderfully true. The Bible book of Proverbs has many such important words of wisdom.**

ACTIVITY Divide into teams of three or four. Give each team a sheet of newsprint, a Bible, and marking pens. Ask everyone to write a proverb related to each of the following topics: family, friends, teachers, Jesus, and God. Tell them to look through the book of Proverbs for examples and ideas. Challenge them to do their own creating and not copy something. Share responses.

DEBRIEFING Read Proverbs 6:16–19. Ask:

- What are "haughty" eyes?

- What's the power of a lying tongue?

- What does it mean to shed innocent blood?

- What are the wicked schemes of the heart?

- Why is quickly rushing into evil so disliked by God?

- What's the danger of a false witness who lies against you?

- How do people stir up dissension among one another?

Say: **These seven things are detestable to God. They're all destroyers of the good God desires of us. They stand for everything that is opposite of Jesus. No wonder the writer of Proverbs calls them the things that the Lord hates. What do you think of this list?**

Think about times you have been caught in these dangers. Recall where your help is. Reach out to Jesus and ask Him to lead you away from these temptations. Rely on His forgiveness and life-changing power.

PRAYER STARTER Think of seven things that are the opposite of the Proverbs list. Ask God to bless you with them.

THE WAY TO GOD

MAIN IDEA   There is only one way to God for the Christian and that's through Jesus.

SCRIPTURE   John 14:5–6

SUPPLIES   Two blindfolds, chairs, paper, and pencils.

INTRODUCTION   Give each person a sheet of paper and a pencil. Tell them to draw a map that leads from your meeting area to their home. Don't put street names on the maps. Gather the maps together and then hold up each map and ask the group to try and guess where it leads.

Say: **It's important to give good directions to people if we want them to come visit us. God gives us good directions on how to be with Him.**

ACTIVITY   Divide into two teams. Set up a row of chairs about six feet apart in front of each team. Give a blindfold to each team and tell them to put it on one member. On *GO,* each team will start yelling directions to the blindfolded person to weave in and out of the chairs and back to the group again. The blindfolded person cannot reach out and touch any of the chairs. Ask:

● What was hard about communicating with your teammate?

● What would have made your job easier?

Try the activity again. This time have the blindfolded person hold onto another person who will lead them through the maze.

DEBRIEFING   Read John 14:5–6. Ask:

● Why do you think Thomas asked Jesus that question?

● What do you think it means to come to God through Jesus?

Say: **Jesus didn't mince words when He responded to Thomas' question. What He said was direct and straight. Make no mistake about it, Jesus told us He is the only way to God. He's the truthful way, and when we follow Him, we find the real meaning of life. And through Jesus we have eternal life. When we meet Jesus, we meet God. It's that simple. Knowing Jesus means knowing God. To be in the presence of God's holiness is as close as your relationship with Jesus.**

PRAYER STARTER   Thank Jesus that He lovingly leads us. Pray that He will give us faith and strength to follow Him.

A FRUITFUL HARVEST

MAIN IDEA Only when we're attached to Christ can we bear fruit.

SCRIPTURE John 15:5–8

SUPPLIES A long, strong rope; newsprint; and marking pens.

INTRODUCTION Ask group members to name all the organizations they are associated with. Make a list on newsprint.

Say: **These groups have a major influence on you. They form a lot of your identity. What we're attached to often determines who we will be.**

ACTIVITY Divide into two teams and tell them to take hold of opposite ends of the rope. Announce that there will be a tug-of-war contest to see which team is the strongest. However, you are going to change how the game is played. Keep score by rounds.

Round 1: Tell everyone on Team A to drop the rope. Ask them to elect one person to do their tugging. Play the round.

Round 2: Tell half of Team A to join their one player. Play the round.

Round 3: Tell all of Team A to join in. Play the round.

Discuss with the group:

● What determined whether your team could play its best?

DEBRIEFING Read John 15:5–8. Ask:

● Are you part of the vine of Jesus or do all the other groups you participate in matter more?

● What happens to those who are apart from Christ?

● How does Jesus' word remain in us?

● What kind of fruit brings glory to God? (See Galatians 5:22–23.)

Say: **When Team A was playing without everyone, it was a pretty weak effort. The other team was overpowering. That happens with us. Unless we're attached to Jesus, the evil stuff in life defeats us. When we're firmly attached to Jesus, the power of the Holy Spirit, working through God's Word and the Sacraments, works in us to help us grow and be strong as people of God.**

PRAYER STARTER Praise God that He willingly and lovingly empowers you with faith and strength to live as His people.

STANDING UP TO THE CROWD

MAIN IDEA   Clothed in His armor, God promises to help us stand firm in the faith in every situation.

SCRIPTURE   Ephesians 6:14–15

SUPPLIES   A variety of shoes that teens would wear for different occasions: sports shoes, dress shoes, casual shoes, slippers, sandals, etc. Small slips of paper and pencils.

INTRODUCTION   Say: **We find ourselves standing in the middle of lots of different crowds on lots of different occasions. Sometimes we feel pretty comfortable standing up for our Christian beliefs. At other times, we might be tempted to go along with the crowd.**

ACTIVITY   Display the shoes in front of the group. Ask each person to write down a temptation to follow the crowd that might come his or her way when wearing each type of shoe. A person wearing a soccer shoe might be tempted to cheat, a person wearing a dress shoe might be tempted to go out and drink, etc. Have the group drop their slips of paper into the appropriate shoes. Ask:

● Have you faced temptations similar to the ones you put in the shoes?

● When is it easiest to give in to sin? Does it depend on where you are and who you're with?

● Is it sometimes easier to go along with the crowd than to stick up for what you believe in?

DEBRIEFING   Read Ephesians 6:14–15. Say: **In these words God describes the armor we wear as Christian warriors. We stand firm with the belt of truth buckled around us—the truth that Jesus died to pay for our sins and that He strengthens us to resist temptation. We are covered with the breastplate of righteousness—the righteousness God places over us at our Baptism as He gives us faith and forgives our sins. Our feet are fitted with sturdy boots, ready to take us through every temptation and trouble with Christ at our side.**

As you find yourself wearing different shoes in different places, think about the armor that God gives you. He'll help you stand up to any crowd and stand firm in the faith.

PRAYER STARTER   Ask God to clothe you in His armor and help you stand firm in every situation.

JUST ONE VOICE

MAIN IDEA   God can work through us to make a difference in this world.

SCRIPTURE   1 Kings 18:17–40

SUPPLIES   Paper, tape, and marking pens.

INTRODUCTION   Ask members to identify people who they think are dangerous. Say: **Everywhere we go, we're going to run into people and groups that are dangerous and exploitive. What can we do about it?**

ACTIVITY   Ask for three volunteers from the group. Tape one of these three signs on each of them: Ridicule, Mean, Snob. Place them at different locations around the room and tell them to stand absolutely rigid with arms tightly at their sides. The first volunteer should repeatedly chant, "That's stupid!" The second person chants, "Get out of my way!" The third chants, "I'm better than you!"

Divide into three groups. Assign each group to one of the statue volunteers. Tell the three groups to figure out a way to counteract their evil statue. Note that attacking evil with evil doesn't counteract it, it multiplies evil. Discuss possible responses and reactions.

DEBRIEFING   Give a little background into Elijah's life as a prophet. Read 1 Kings 18:17–40. Ask:

● What do you think it would have been like to be with Elijah on the mountain that day?

● Why do you think Elijah was willing to stand up against 450 idol-worshiping prophets?

● When was a time you acted like Elijah and stood against great odds for what you believed?

Say: **Elijah was only one voice among 450 evil men. He stood alone. He was not willing for the people to be lured into idol worship any further. He put his life on the line. How could one person be so brave? How could one person make such a difference? The answer is that it wasn't the power of one person, it was the power of the one true God working through him.**

Every day each of us can stand up for God in some way. It's going to be hard. Sometimes you will be the only voice of sanity. You might be the only one trying to stamp out ridicule and meanness and snobbery. But you can do it as you rely on God to forgive your failures, trust in Him to make you strong, and follow Him with faith commitment.

PRAYER STARTER   Pray that God will help each of you be a voice for God even when it's hard to do so.

WHAT IS HUMILITY?

MAIN IDEA   Jesus leads us to serve others with humility.

SCRIPTURE   John 13:1–17

SUPPLIES   Newsprint, marking pens, a bowl of water, a towel, and a candle.

INTRODUCTION   Ask group members to give examples of arrogant and of humble behaviors. Write the responses on newsprint.

Say: **It's hard to be humble. There seems to be a voice inside us that says we should be proud and boastful rather than gentle and humble. Jesus knew a lot about what humility means.**

ACTIVITY   Sit in a circle. Place a candle in the center of the group. Ask group members to take off their shoes and socks. Take a bowl of warm water and ask each group member to wash the feet of the person on their right. As they are doing it, talk about Jesus' last meal with His disciples.

DEBRIEFING   Read John 13:1–17. Ask:

● Why do you think Peter asked Jesus not to wash his feet?

● How did you feel about washing someone's feet?

● What's the real purpose for foot washing?

Say: **How incredible that experience must have been for the disciples. Here was their Lord washing their feet. You see, the King of Kings and Lord of Lords knelt down and washed His disciples dirty and smelly feet. He didn't consider Himself greater than others, but He willingly came to save, to serve, and to teach us. Always remember that Jesus takes us to our knees with Him to wash the feet of those we think inferior.**

PRAYER STARTER Pray that God will forgive boastful pride and lead each of you to a humble spirit.

A NEW CREATION

MAIN IDEA When we are in Christ, we are turned into someone new.

SCRIPTURE 2 Corinthians 5:17

SUPPLIES Marking pens and newsprint.

INTRODUCTION Ask the group to tell you some of the new things they have received or done in the past year. Ask which one has been their favorite and why.

Say: **We all like to get and do new things. We somehow feel better. We get excited.**

ACTIVITY Give each person a marking pen and a sheet of newsprint. Tell them to draw an outline of a person to represent themselves. Inside that outline, have them write five things they'd like to change about themselves. In other words, how would they give themselves a makeover?

When everyone finishes share the makeover lists. Ask:

● In what ways would you be someone new if those things happened?

● Which of those five things is the most important to you?

DEBRIEFING Read 2 Corinthians 5:17. Ask:

● What do you think it means to become a new creation through Christ?

● What has Christ done to get rid of your old sinful self?

● How might Jesus radically change your life so you are nothing like before?

Say: **Scripture promises that Jesus does transform us. With Christ, you get a new you. Through our Lord and Savior's forgiveness and transforming power, we're promised a new beginning. We become a new creation with all of the potential and promises God has for us. Through Jesus we become heirs of the kingdom of God. Let go of the old you if it's keeping you from knowing the fullness of Christ. Jesus offers you a complete makeover—not in looks but in life. Claim the power of Christ.**

PRAYER STARTER Thank God that He forgives your old sinful self and leads you to new attitudes, new ways, new lives.

THE CONTAGIOUS CHURCH

MAIN IDEA   The power of the Holy Spirit can bless us as a church family.

SCRIPTURE   Acts 2:41–47

SUPPLIES   Newsprint and marking pens.

INTRODUCTION   Ask the group to tell you some of the childhood diseases they caught. What do they remember about them? Write their comments on newsprint.

Say: **It's easy to catch a cold, the mumps, or chicken pox because they're contagious. God would like us to be a faith-filled community of believers in a church that others find contagious.**

ACTIVITY   Divide into small groups. Give each one newsprint and marking pens. Tell them to list as many things as they can that are good about their church. Share results. Ask:

- What do you think is the best quality of your church?

- How do you think the church got it?

- What would you like to change about your church?

DEBRIEFING   Say: **I'm going to read a list of things about a church that was active, growing, and empowered by the Holy Spirit.** Read Acts 2:42–47. Ask:

- What were some of the characteristics of the early Christian church?

- What do you think it means that everyone was filled with awe?

- If you had been part of that early church, what would you have wanted to learn from the apostles?

- What do you think it would be like to be around people who always have glad and sincere hearts?

- What was God doing in the hearts of the early Christians and in their community?

Say: **The early church was a contagious place. It was more powerful than any contagious disease. Those early Christians had a fiery faith that was dominated by their love for Jesus. They knew He had done something remarkable through His death and resurrection. They were praise-filled people. Perhaps we need an extra measure of this contagious spirit in our church and in our youth group. Through the power of the Holy Spirit, this can happen.**

PRAYER STARTER   Pray that Christ will send the Holy Spirit to enliven and enrich your church and your group.

DON'T HIDE THE PRIDE

MAIN IDEA   Jesus wants us to be proud of His Gospel and never ashamed to share it with others.

SCRIPTURE   Romans 1:16–17

SUPPLIES   Newsprint and marking pens.

INTRODUCTION   Ask the group to tell you things they have done that they are proud of. Ask them to tell you the people in their lives that they are proud of.

Say: **While one type of pride can be self-centered and hurtful, another type of pride rejoices in recognizing and appreciating the blessings God gives us. We can be proud of our accomplishments and we can be proud of others because these are gifts from God. We can also take pride in our great and faithful God Himself.**

ACTIVITY   Divide the group into pairs and have the pairs face each other. One at a time, the partners should pick someone in their lives and describe why they are proud of that person.

Gather together and discuss individual answers. Make a list of things on newsprint that seem to be a common thread in this arena of pride. Ask:

- What must someone do for you to be proud of them?

- What are some things you have done to make a parent proud of you?

DEBRIEFING   Read Romans 1:16–17. Ask:

- Why do you think Paul was so proud of the Gospel?

- When was the last time you were ashamed of something or someone?

- When you are proud of something or someone, what do you usually do?

Say: **Are you proud of the Gospel of Jesus Christ? Are you proud to let everyone know that you are indeed a Christian? Where can you get the powerful pride to stand up in the face of wrong as Jesus would have done? Where can you get the courageous pride to put your life into Jesus' hands in a risky situation? Listen again to Romans 1:16–17. Never be ashamed to call on the name of Jesus.**

PRAYER STARTER   Pray that God will help each of you have pride in the Gospel and always share it with others.

GIVE OF YOURSELF

MAIN IDEA   Jesus can take what we offer Him and turn it into something fabulous.

SCRIPTURE   John 6:1–13

SUPPLIES   None.

INTRODUCTION   Sit in a circle. Ask the group to think about the people in the room. Go around the circle and respond to: "The best gift someone in this room has given me is … "

Say: **We don't really know the little parts of ourselves we share and give to others. But they remember them. When we give a little of ourselves to Jesus, He blesses it and multiplies it.**

ACTIVITY   Put a chair in the center of the group. Ask a volunteer to sit in that chair. Starting with the person on your left, go around the circle and have each group member tell the person in the middle what they appreciate most about him or her. Make sure everyone sits in the chair, even if they're shy. Ask:

● How do you feel after hearing what your friends appreciate about you?

● Why was it uncomfortable for some of you to receive those compliments?

● What happens to people when we build them up?

● What will each of you remember about this experience?

DEBRIEFING   Read John 6:1–13. Ask:

● If you had been that little boy, what would you have done if Jesus asked to use your meal?

● What are some things you are willing to give to Jesus to use?

Say: **A little boy trusted Jesus with his supper. It was something small, but Jesus turned it into enough food to feed thousands. Who would have ever thought that was possible? We may ask, "What do I have that I can give?" We see our sins and weaknesses and failures. But Jesus comes with forgiveness, power, and blessing to transform us.**

Jesus can take your words and thoughts and actions and work miracles. He takes our hearts so He can win others through us. He sharpens our intellects to know Him better. He lives in us so He can help us grow as His dear children. Oh, the miracles He can fashion in your life!

PRAYER STARTER   Pray that God will help each of you fully live out your faith in Jesus.